African Fiction
and Joseph Conrad

African Fiction
and Joseph Conrad

Reading Postcolonial Intertextuality

Byron Caminero-Santangelo

State University of New York Press

Published by
State University of New York Press, Albany

© 2005 State University of New York

For information, address State University of New York Press,
90 State Street, Suite 700, Albany, NY 12207

Production by Michael Haggett
Marketing by Anne M. Valentine

Library of Congress Cataloging-in-Publication Data

Caminero-Santangelo, Byron, 1961–
  Reading postcolonial intertextuality : African fiction and Joseph Conrad / Byron
Caminero-Santangelo.
    p. cm.
  Includes bibliographical references and index.
  ISBN 0-7914-6261-7 (hardcover : alk. paper) — ISBN 0-7914-6262-5 (pbk. : alk. paper)
  1. Conrad, Joseph, 1857–1924—Criticism and interpretation. 2. Literature,
Comparative—English and African. 3. Literature, Comparative—African and English. 4.
African fiction—History and criticism. 5. Postcolonialism in literature. 6.
Postcolonialism—Africa. 7. Africa—In literature. 8. Intertextuality. I. Title.
  PR6005.O4Z5695 2004
  828'.912—dc22

                                                                              2004013798

10 9 8 7 6 5 4 3 2 1

#55729719

For Marta, Nicola, and Gabriel

Contents

Acknowledgments

Many thanks to editor Jane Bunker and production editor Michael Haggett, who have been very helpful and easy to work with throughout the publication process.

Earlier versions of portions of this book appeared in other publications. I thank the editors for permission to include these sections in revised form: "Subjects in History: Disruptions of the Colonial in *Heart of Darkness* and *July's People*," in *Conrad at the Millennium: Modernism, Postmodernism, Postcolonialism*, edited by Gail Fincham and Attie DeLange, Social Science Monographs/Curie-Sklodowska University/Columbia University Press, 2001, 427–452; "Legacies of Darkness: Neo-colonialism, Conrad, and Salih's *Season of Migration to the North*," in *Ariel: A Review of International English Literature* 30.4 (1999): 7–33; "Neo-colonialism and the Betrayal Plot in *A Grain of Wheat*: Ngugi wa Thiong'o's Re-Vision of *Under Western Eyes*," in *Research in African Literatures* 29.1 (1998): 139–152.

Offering careful readings, helpful advice, and/or stimulating discussion, many friends and colleagues have been instrumental in the production of this book: Giselle Anatol, Chima Anyadike, David Bergeron, Pete Casagrande, Laura Chrisman, Katie Conrad, Dorice Elliott, Joseph Harrington, George Hartley, Garth Myers, Joel Reed, Elizabeth Shultz, and Simon Lewis. Dick Hardin and Jim Hartman, in their tenures as chair of English, gave me crucial institutional (and emotional) support. Thanks also to the University of Kansas General Research Fund for summer support in the writing of two of the chapters and to the University's African Studies Center which helped fund my trips to conferences where I presented sections of this project.

I am forever indebted to J. Hillis Miller who taught me that reading a literary text should be a continuously challenging endeavor and whose encouragement and support allowed me to develop as a scholar in my own way. He guided me through my dissertation on Conrad (which laid some of the groundwork for this project) and helped me to understand what a mentor can and should be.

My parents, Beth and Jerry Santangelo, raised me in an intellectually stimulating environment and instilled in me a love of books as well as a strong sense of social and intellectual commitment. They also furnished me with financial and emotional support when I needed it and guided me with excellent advice. There really is no way for me to express my gratitude to them adequately.

Thanks and love also to Whitney Santangelo and the Camineros who have offered me various kinds of support throughout the years and to Nicola and Gabriel who have helped me to keep my scholarship and career in perspective and made me laugh.

Thanks most of all to Marta, who has read and reread the chapters of this book countless times and without whose encouragement and help it quite literally would not have been written. She has been my intellectual and emotional anchor.

INTRODUCTION

Beyond Writing Back

Alternative Uses of Postcolonial Cultural Hybridity

For reasons both good and bad, the study of postcolonial hybridity remains tied to a typology which defines postcolonial cultures in terms of their oppositional relationship with the West. Recent postcolonial theory certainly rejects the notion of autonomous, static collective identities associated with both colonial ideology and certain nativist forms of anti-colonial nationalism in favor of a vision of interdependent and overlapping cultures which breaks from essentialist formulations of cultural difference. As a result this theory often privileges postcolonial cultural production, which reflects what Edward Said calls the "voyage in": "the conscious effort to enter into the discourse of Europe and the West, to mix with it, transform it" (216) and thereby undermine the idea "that there is an 'us' and a 'them,' each quite settled, clear, unassailably self-evident" (xxv). Yet as conceived by many critics and theorists, the voyage in still locks postcolonial hybridity into the same underlying oppositional binary assumed by nativism. Despite the notion of a challenge to clearly distinguished identities, the revision of Western cultural forms is conceptualized as a strategy to establish an oppositional voice by invoking and challenging the imperial vision supposedly embedded in the heart of Western culture. In other words, the postcolonial remains defined in terms of a battle between colonial European and anticolonial, non-Western cultures.

As some critics note, the notion that postcolonial cultures are defined by attempts to undermine assumptions of the West obscures an incredible spectrum of political concerns. For example, such a focus elides the various forms of collective identity stressed by recent internal and national colonial relations. That is to say, postcolonial cultural production should be interpreted in terms of the effort to create oppositional positions and voices, *not* by countering a single, transhistorical European colonial ideology, but by engaging with a wide range of historically specific national and transnational ideologies. This study examines many discontinuous functions cultural syncretism serves when appropriations of Western cultural forms are interpreted in relation to the wide variety of political and cultural concerns within the postcolonial world. I suggest that the set of relations between Western and postcolonial cultures entailed by hybridity is much more complex than has been implied by the focus on parodic revision. Ultimately, this study resists representations of the Western and the Postcolonial as opponents forever engaged in the same battle. Rather it insists on questioning formulations of such clearly delineated, oppositional cultural categories and rehistoricizing the objects of study, including the complex process of cultural exchange.

The conception of postcolonial hybridity embraced by recent postcolonial theory is particularly apparent in discussions of the relationships between European and postcolonial literatures. This theory focuses extensively on the way the European canon and its study serve the interests of empire by reinforcing the forms of identity posited by colonial discourse. Concomitantly, there is a notion of postcolonial cultures that defines them in terms of "a textual contest, or a bibliographic battle, between oppressive and subversive books" (Ghandi 141), in which European literature represents the former and postcolonial writing the latter. When combined with postcolonial theory's preference for appropriation of Western cultural forms rather than an essentialist rejection of Western culture (what *The Empire Writes Back* labels "abrogation"[38]), the notion of this battle leads to a particular focus on the way that intentional hybridity in postcolonial literatures—understood as the inappropriate appropriation of Western literary language, conventions, and texts—enables a particularly effective form of writing back to the imperial center. Thus, the rewritings of canonical Western literature are primary examples of the anticolonial voyage in. The assumption that postcolonial writers revise canonical European literary texts in order to challenge European colonial ideology is so pervasive that it persists in innumerable readings of postcolonial literatures and theoretical discussions of postcolonial textuality.

The relationships between African fiction and Joseph Conrad's "classics" offer particularly fertile ground to interrogate the notion of the voyage in advocated by most postcolonial theorists, and to explore alternatives. Conrad's work is often represented as embodying the colonial canon to which postcolonial writers write back. Probably the literary "classic" most associated with a Western vision of Africa, *Heart of Darkness* features prominently in critical discussions of African writers' efforts to discredit the image of Africa drawn by colonial discourse. Many critics are quick to assert that Conrad's novella embraces a colonialist perspective; perhaps the most commonly cited example is Marlow's representation of Africans dancing on the banks of the Congo, in which he attributes his incomprehension to evolutionary distance and to a kind of madness resulting from their prehistoric close association with the deadly and chaotic jungle:

> But suddenly as we struggled round a bend there would be a glimpse of rush walls, of peaked grass roofs, a burst of yells, a whirl of black limbs, a mass of hands clapping, of feet stamping, of bodies swaying, of eyes rolling under the droop of heavy and motionless foliage. The steamer toiled along slowly on the edge of a black and incomprehensible frenzy. The prehistoric man was cursing us, praying to us, welcoming us—who could tell? We were cut off from the comprehension of our surroundings; we glided past like phantoms, wondering and secretly appalled, as sane men would be before an enthusiastic outbreak in a madhouse. We could not understand because we were too far and could not remember because we were traveling in the night of first ages, of those ages that are gone, leaving hardly a sign—and no memories. (37)

It is certainly true that despite his moments of doubt and liberal sympathies Marlow frequently depicts Africans in these clichéd terms; he never rejects the image of natives as a people without civilization or culture who, in comparison with Europeans, are little more than animals. In his famous essay, *Image of Africa,* Chinua Achebe insists that Conrad's vision of Africa is identical to Marlow's. Achebe uses this passage along with many others to argue that *Heart of Darkness* reinforces Western assumptions about Africa and Africans and that Conrad himself is a "thorough going racist" (*Hopes* 11). That the book's canonical status remains unaffected by its racism is evidence, according to Achebe, of how deeply rooted those assumptions are in the Western psyche.

With this view of Conrad in mind, many critics assume that numerous Conradian echoes in novels by some of the most prominent anticolonial authors from Africa—including Achebe, Ngugi, Gordimer, Salih, and Aidoo—are key examples of subversive appropriation in which postcolonial writers revise European classics in order to engage those classics in a critical dialogue and to undermine the colonial ur-narrative embedded in them. For example, in *Culture and Imperialism,* Said suggests that postcolonial African authors' appropriations of Conrad both highlight how the Western classic has been determined by imperial "structures of attitude and reference" and undermine these "structures" (xxiii). Of course this notion of intertextual combat is widely disseminated using other examples of literary intertextuality—for example, the many appropriations of *The Tempest* by Caribbean authors; however, the echoes of Conrad in African fiction remain, by far, the most popular examples drawn from African literature.

Although there is little doubt the model of combative postcolonial intertextuality offers important insights into some African literature, the following study of the relationships between African novels and Conrad's fiction departs significantly from a number of its assumptions and highlights some of its limitations. Instead of focusing on how African novels write back to the colonial perspective associated with Conrad's fiction and disrupt the imperial relations of power which that perspective reinforces, this study examines how African novels address different forms of colonial power and discourse generated by the history of national independence and the development of the postcolonial nation. In other words, the significance of the intertextual relationship is not primarily determined by how (and whether) the Conradian intertext embodies the colonial narrative of his place and time, since this is not the primary narrative which the African novel seeks to counter. Rather, significance is determined by how Conradian elements are relevant to the effort by African novels to intervene in specific repressive (often neocolonial) situations in late twentieth-century postcolonial Africa and how those elements are transformed in the process. I do not dispute the claim, made by many postcolonial critics and theorists, that such appropriations disrupt the principles underlying colonial epistemology by undermining notions of autonomous cultural traditions and identities. However, a focus on writing back results in eliding the varied foci and concerns of African fiction and can vastly simplify the purposes of the intertextual relationships with European literature. These relationships are not always—in fact are often not— about writing back to the West or to the colonial archive. My approach also does not represent the African novels as less anticolonial, original, or powerful because they are drawing on Conrad's fiction without being focused on attacking it. In fact, quite the opposite: their power is to be found precisely in their ability to appropriate and transform Conradian intertexts and make them relevant to their socially and historically specific concerns.

The notion that African literature writes back to a European colonial literary tradition can be partly traced to the focus on a number of seminal African novels which helped inaugurate a tradition of African writing. In an effort to restore a positive sense of community and culture on which a postcolonial future could be built, some of the most important writers from the era of anticolonial nationalism set out to challenge what Abdulrazak Gurnah calls "the self-righteous narrative of imperial advance" which offered the following image of "a passive and largely oblivious Africa": "While industrious and resourceful Europeans built railways and opened up waterways, despite the often fatal harshness of conditions, ignorant Africans slumbered on in their 'night of first ages' until shaken awake and forced into the light by European intervention" (Gurnah x). (Gurnah's passing reference to *Heart of Darkness* ['night of first ages'] exemplifies the frequent connection between Conrad's novella and imperial ideology in discussions of African literature.) Authors such as Chinua Achebe were exposed to the colonial narrative in its most carefully crafted form in the literature the colonial educational system required them to read, and, as a result, they often wrote back to that narrative's manifestations in the European canon.[1] Achebe, for example, claims that the origin of his literary career is to be found in a desire to counter the image of Africa that runs through British literature as exemplified by *Heart of Darkness:*

> I went to the first university that was built in Nigeria, and I took a course in English. We were taught the same kind of literature that British people were taught in their own university. But then I began to look at these books in a different light. When I had been younger, I had read these adventure books about the good white man, you know, wandering into the jungle or into danger, and the savages were after him. And I would instinctively be on the side of the white man. You see what fiction can do, it can put you on the wrong side if you are not developed enough. In the university I suddenly saw that these books had to be read in a different light. Reading *Heart of Darkness,* for instance, which was a very, very highly praised book and which is still highly praised, I realized that I was one of those savages jumping up and down on

the beach. Once that kind of Enlightenment comes to you, you
realize that someone has to write a different story. And since I was
in any case inclined that way, why not me? (Moyers 343)

Achebe's representation of his writing rings especially true for *Things Fall
Apart*, which is clearly part of a paradigm that, as Gurnah pithily comments, can "be summarized as: ignorant accounts of Africa written by
arrogant Europeans were followed by insider accounts that wrote back to
them" (ix). *Things Fall Apart* signals its effort to write back to the European colonial narrative in numerous ways—the most glaring of which is
the final chapter in which Achebe takes on the voice of the District Com-
missioner in order to dialogically undermine the colonial point of view.
Further, the novel echoes moments of *Heart of Darkness* itself, investing
those echoes with new and inverted meanings. In Conrad's novella, the
sound of drums embodies the spirit of Africa; as such, it is at best an
enigma and at worst the sound of the corrosive and deadly darkness itself.
In *Things Fall Apart*, as the sound of the life of the village, the sound of
drums reflects the communal and cultural power enabling the Igbo to
tame and control the deadly forces of nature, which is one manifestation
of the darkness in Conrad's novel. These aspects of *Things Fall Apart*
encourage a reading of it in terms of the effort to write back to Western
classics such as *Heart of Darkness* and, thereby, to disrupt the visions of
colonialism and Africa they can be read as reinforcing.[2] The prominence
of works like *Things Fall Apart* in the canon of African literature has
fueled and given legitimacy to the notion of a tradition which runs
counter to a European literary tradition.

The impetus to create such an oppositional disjunction also stems
from an effort by critics and theorists to challenge the notions of African
literature offered by European literary critics. Such critics were generally
heavily influenced by a colonial discourse that denied the existence of
African literary traditions and suggested Africans needed to be instructed
by European literary masterpieces if they were to develop a proper literature of their own. As a result, they judged written literature produced by
Africans in terms of the degree to which its authors properly used the
forms and reflected the values embedded in European traditions, at least
as they were constructed by European criticism. Just as important, these
critics focused on the ways African literary production was the result of
European influence (especially if it was deemed "good"). As Chidi Amuta
claims, "African literary genius [. . .] must have been catalyzed by the
'benefits' of the so-called European civilizing mission in Africa. Thus, the

endless quest for European influences on African writers is one of the ruses in the trick bags of members of this formation" (19). In this way, African literature is represented as a kind of "junior brother" or stepchild to a great and powerful European literary tradition: "Camara Laye was, above all, the heir of Kafka, Achebe of Conrad, Sembene of Zola, Senghor of Claudel and Saint John Perse, and so on. Eurocentric views of African literature did not stop at intertextuality and affinity; they appropriated African literature and 'colonized' it completely" (Julien 3–4).[3]

This representation of the relationship between the two literary traditions is underpinned by European notions of national literatures and relationships of influence among them. As Kwame Appiah points out, when the conception of the racialized nation was connected with the Herderian notion that each nation shared a culture and, especially, a language and literature, "we arrive at the racial understanding of literature that flourishes from the mid-nineteenth century in the work of the first modern literary historians" (51).[4] These historians attempt to unearth the moral and intellectual essence at the heart of a nation's literature in order to determine that nation's proper place "in the order of moral and intellectual endowments" (51). The strength and value of a national literary tradition and, consequently, of a nation's essence is determined by the degree to which that tradition remained autonomous from the influence of other literary traditions. At the same time, it is believed powerful and original literary traditions not only shape their own masterpieces, but also help other peoples and their literatures to evolve; evidence of literary influence is proof on the one hand of the value of the influential culture and on the other of the dependence and inferiority of the culture being influenced. According to Jay Clayton and Eric Rothstein, "discovering parallels between the literature of two nations was put to the service of a crude cultural imperialism; a work, a movement, or an entire national literature was exalted to the degree that it was able to exert a hegemony over the literature of other countries" (5). Given the history of colonialist criticism and its connection with these nationalist conceptions of literature and literary influence, it is not surprising that literary critics concerned with the project of decolonization and the threat of cultural recolonization de-emphasized affiliation and emphasized opposition in their approach to the relationship between European and African literature. Cultural decolonization seems to necessitate a challenge to any suggestion of the dependence of African literature on the European canon by focusing on how African writing opposes the assumptions embedded in that canon and breaks from its values.

The oppositional conception of the relationship between the two traditions often takes on a nativist tinge. The nativist critic asserts African literature is based on an authentic African worldview, aesthetics, and set of values which are utterly autonomous from those offered by Western literature:

> traditionalist aestheticians of African literature have relentlessly invoked a certain amorphously defined "African world view" as the informing metaphysical bedrock of their postulations. As it is popularized and bandied around by anthropologists, religionists and professional philosophers, *the* African world view refers to an absolute, fairly homogenous, immutable and eternal mode of perceiving reality and explaining phenomena by which Africa can be distinguished from the West in particular. (Amuta 38)

The earliest and most famous proponents of nativist notions of African culture were the poets and philosophers of Negritude. These notions, however, remain extremely durable. In the eighties, nativism's most aggressive proponents were the so-called bolekaja critics Chinweizu, Jemie, and Madubuike who wrote the well-known manifesto *Toward the Decolonization of African Literature,* in which they assert cultural decolonization necessitates African literature use African orature "as the ultimate foundation, guidepost, and point of departure" since it "is the incontestable reservoir of the values, sensibilities, aesthetics, and achievements of traditional African thought and imagination" (2). These critics exhort African authors to struggle against "the perverted fascination with and emulation of Western literature" (3). In the bolekaja school of thought, European literary influence is dangerous for African literature because of possible infection by European sensibility and must be avoided by grounding the literary work in formal African elements. As expected, little commentary on the connections between African fiction and Conrad comes from nativist critics since they strive to downplay the impact of Western literature on African literary production. When such critics do mention these connections, they stress the marginal importance of Conrad for the central concerns and perspective of the African text, and/or they suggest there is a danger in appropriations of Conrad's fiction as a result of the possibility of infection by Western values.

In his attack on Negritude and its ilk, Frantz Fanon in *The Wretched of the Earth* anticipated many of the accusations leveled at nativism by more recent Marxist and postcolonial critics. Fanon asserts Negritude is a kind of ideological false consciousness which represses the impact of history and the existence of diverse social contexts by offering the fairytale of a homogenous and ahistorical African culture which, if embraced, will lead to decolonization and a bright postcolonial future. Echoing Fanon's assertion that this fairytale will lead "men of African culture [. . .] up a blind alley," the Marxist critic Chidi Amuta claims there is "a basic reluctance on the part of [nativist] scholars to see Africa not only as part of a changing world but also as a highly heterogenous and multivalent geopolitical entity whose problems need to be confronted at the level of theories with practical value for both the present and future" (Amatu 35). According to Fanon, the nativist conception of an African culture results from what Spivak calls repetition-in-rupture; the effort to counter the colonialist myth is still caught within the false conceptions of racial identity underpinning that myth:

> Colonialism's condemnation is continental in its scope. The contention by colonialism that the darkest night of humanity lay over pre-colonial history concerns the whole of the African continent. The efforts of the native to rehabilitate himself and to escape from the claws of colonialism are logically inscribed from the same point of view as that of colonialism. [. . .] The Negro, never so much a Negro as since he has been dominated by the whites, when he decides to prove that he has a culture and to behave like a cultured person, comes to realize that history points out a well-defined path to him: he must demonstrate that a Negro culture exists. (212)

Expanding on Fanon's argument by tracing the links between the philosophical underpinnings of nativism and the Western ideology of national literature, Kwame Appiah claims nativist literary critics bought into Western representations of racial essences embedded in literary traditions: "defiance is determined less by 'indigenous' notions of resistance than by the dictates of the West's own Herderian legacy—its highly elaborated ideologies of national autonomy, of language and literature as cultural substrate [. . .] few things, then, are less native than nativism in its current forms" (59–60).

Critics like Appiah are especially concerned that by buying into Western nationalist ideology, nativism suppresses the contingent and heterogenous construction of culture and identity. They claim it forecloses on the possibility that African voices could appear through the revision of

European literary form and that the use of European elements by African authors could itself be a potently subversive means of undermining colonial discourse (particularly its construction of racial and geographic identities). Writing of a similar situation in African-American literature, Henry Louis Gates argues the power and originality of masterful revision was long repressed by Black writers and critics who struggled "under the burden of avoiding repetition, revision, or reinterpretation" because of the racist assertion that those of African descent lacked any capacity for literary originality and could only be mimics. Failing to recognize "the distinction between originality and imitation is a false distinction," these writers and critics succumb "to a political argument that reflects a racist subtext" and remained locked into the architecture of literature and race imposed by Euro-American thought (118).

Implicitly or explicitly acknowledging the transformative and productive power in the process of rewriting to which Gates refers, the majority of critics commenting on African authors' appropriations of Conrad's work with a model of African/European intertextuality based on the notion of parodic or critical revision.[5] Celebrated by a number of prominent postcolonial theorists, this model represents postcolonial authors as echoing European literary classics in order to engage them in an oppositional dialogue and, through this dialogue, disrupt the colonial vision and epistemology these classics reflect and legitimate. As the authors of *Decolonising Fictions* claim:

> The relation of the postcolonial text to its [European] thematic ancestors is often parodic. As Linda Hutchean points out, parody may be "repetition with critical distance, which marks difference rather than similarity." In the postcolonial context, parody often establishes a dialogue where first there was only monologue. When Caliban, Ariel, Miranda, and Friday "talk back," a new configuration emerges. (Brydon 89)

In one sense, this perspective on literary influence subscribes to a Bloomian model, which recognizes the construction of identity in difference through the literary text's misreading of its intertextual other, and its creation of its own original voice through the distortion and transformation of the earlier text. Yet, it avoids the ahistorical orientation of the Bloomian model because this perspective acknowledges the importance of other, non-literary kinds of texts for the development of the differential voice (and, thus, counters the Bloomian notion that a piece of literature only ever really takes its significance from its Oedipal relationships with other literary texts). As Bart Moore-Gilbert notes, postcolonial theory in general insists "upon the importance of studying literature together with history, politics, sociology, and other art forms rather than in isolation from the multiple material and intellectual contexts which determine its production and reception" (8). The voice of the postcolonial author comes out not just through the revision of the European classic, but, just as important, through its engagement with the larger social (colonial) text that supposedly speaks through the classic.

The focus on the connection between literary texts and a broader cultural or social textuality suggests the notion of parodic revision postulated in postcolonial studies is actually much more closely linked to Bakhtinian dialogism than to Bloomian notions of literary influence. Bakhtinian dialogism and the concepts of intertextuality Kristeva and others have developed from it suggest literary texts are shot through with a variety of social and cultural codes in relation to which they take their meaning in dialogue. As Kristeva notes, "Bakhtin situates the text within history and society, which are seen as texts read by the writer, and into which he inserts himself by rewriting them" (65). Resulting from the transformative dialogue between the literary text and the variety of texts it appropriates, all literary meaning lies on the border between it and its intertextual others. Writing of "an insight first introduced into literary theory by Bakhtin," Kristeva claims "any text is a construction as a mosaic of quotations; any text is the absorption and transformation of another" (66). The basic principles of Bakhtinian dialogism are clearly at work when theorists and critics discuss how postcolonial authors create their own voices through a process of parodic "absorption and transformation" of Western classics and the colonial discourse they represent.

This form of intertextuality is often touted by literary critics as a means of critiquing the notion of clearly distinguished, static collective identities shared both by imperialism and nativism. For example, in *Culture and Imperialism*, Edward Said claims the revisionary strategy—or what he calls "reinscription"—undermines the idea "that there is an 'us' and a 'them,' each quite settled, clear, unassailably self-evident" (xxv). According to Said, this strategy is part of what he calls the "voyage in" which involves the effort by the formerly colonized "to rechart and then occupy the place in imperial cultural forms reserved for subordination, to occupy it self-consciously, fighting for it on the very same territory once ruled by a consciousness that assumed the subordination of a designated inferior" (210). While emphasizing the notion of cultural combat, Said claims the voyage in embraces a vision of interdependent and overlapping cultures and, as a result, breaks from essentialist formulations of cultural difference projected by European colonial and nationalist ideology.[6] Thus, by "breaking down the barriers between cultures" and offering an "alternative" to a colonial conception of collective identity, "reinscription" is more truly anticolonial than nativist efforts to project an opposition between non-European and European cultures in terms of national essences (216). This is a point on which the authors of *The Empire Writes Back* are also emphatic:

> Directly and indirectly, in Salman Rushdie's phrase, the "Empire writes back" to the imperial "centre," not only through nationalist assertion, proclaiming itself central and self-determining, but even more radically by questioning the bases of European and British metaphysics, challenging the world-view that can polarize centre and periphery in the first place. [. . .] Writers such as J.M. Coetzee, Wilson Harris, V.S. Naipaul, George Lamming, Patrick White, Chinua Achebe, Margaret Atwood, and Jean Rhys have all rewritten particular works from the English "canon" with a view to restructuring European "realities" in post-colonial terms, not simply by reversing the hierarchical order, but by interrogating the philosophical assumptions on which that order was based. (33)

Like Said, Ashcroft et al. claim postcolonial revision of Western classics is more radically anti-colonial than nativism because it undermines (rather than reinforces) the dichotomies that underpin colonial culture—including "the English 'canon.'"

However, despite its more hybrid and heterogenous vision of culture, the notion of "reinscription" advocated by Said and *The Empire Writes Back* is based on the typology of writing back. Although it rejects essentialist divisions between literary traditions, it defines the relationship between Western and non-Western literatures in binary, oppositional terms—postcolonial non-Western literary traditions strive to talk back to the Western canon and the colonial vision it represents. Europe's silenced others may now speak in their own "original" voices through a dialogic process of resemblance to and distortion of Western literary discourse and thereby create an apparently hybrid postcolonial literary identity. But that identity is still characterized as unified in its combative opposition to a singular European literary tradition. In fact, for many theorists, the difference between the two is now defined precisely in terms of a split between a monologic, authoritative colonial vision and a subversive, dialogic postcolonial hybridity. For example, Helen Tiffen and Diana Brydon claim that:

> [t]he postcolonial literatures take us from the monocentric into the polyphonic, from the dominance of a single culture into convergent cultures, from pure ancestory into hybridisation, from the novel of persuasion to the novel of carnival. [. . .] The product of mass migrations of the past two centuries, postcolonial fictions help to decolonize our imaginations, by enacting various modes of escape from the mental straitjackets in which imperial habits of mind had locked them. (33)

From this perspective, postcolonial reinscription itself becomes a key means of differentiating postcolonial literature from colonial literature since its dialogism creates voices that "override the single voice of a monocentric discourse, moving them away from the language of traditional English fiction toward a complex interplaying of competing languages" (104). This insistence on oppositional difference—despite the concomitant focus on cultural interdependence and hybridity—is, at least in part, a result of the desire to avoid the notion of influence embraced by colonialist criticism (discussed earlier) in which literary intertextuality is understood in hierarchical terms with the influenced text being placed in a subservient position to the dominant influencing text.[7] In contrast, the writing back approach insists on the need for a reading process focused on establishing difference in order to avoid what critics see as the recolonizing effort reflected in establishing similarity. For instance, Brydon and Tiffen assert "the postcolonial reader seeking to decolonise rather than to recolonise fictions" must use "a reading process that looks for differences rather than similarities" (89).

Despite its best intentions, however, the parodic revisionary model still threatens to colonize postcolonial literatures by characterizing them in terms of their opposition to European colonialism.[8] This formulation homogenizes postcolonial literatures' wide variety of socio-historical concerns by suggesting they are always focused on deconstructing the assumptions of the West. As Arun Mukherjee claims, "This kind of theorizing leaves us only one modality, one discursive position. We are forever forced to interrogate European discourses, of only one particular kind, the ones that degrade and deny our humanity. I would like to respond that our cultural productions are created in response to our own needs, and we have many more needs than constantly to 'parody the imperialists'" (6). Making a similar claim about Fredric Jameson's theorizing of a split in consciousness between "the First World and the Third," Aijaz Ahmed asserts, "Difference between [them] is absolutized as an Otherness, but the enormous cultural heterogeneity of social formations within the so-called Third World is submerged within a singular identity of experience" (*In Theory* 104). Ahmed is particularly concerned with the way looking at "'Third World' literary texts always in terms of their determination by the colonial encounter" suppresses the "fundamental differences within particular national structures—differences, let us say, of class or of gender formation" (92). Even when postcolonial texts do emphasize the issues of colonialism and decolonization, the meanings of these terms cannot be assumed since they are often transformed or at least inflected by the texts' specific social concerns and historical contexts. A focus on a singular imperial formation can result in the evacuation of historical specificity—the erasure of the different dividing lines and types of agency that varied forms and moments of colonialism emphasize. Peter Hulme has made this point in respect to those postcolonial texts which do seem to write back to the imperial center and which do foreground their differences from the Western canon. Discussing the ubiquitous pairing of *Wide Sargasso Sea* and *Jane Eyre,* Hulme claims that if the "pedagogical opposition of the 'colonial' and the 'postcolonial' is allowed to become too fixed, too orthodox a way of organising research projects on books like *Wide Sargasso Sea,* then the critical enterprise risks becoming located at such a high level of generality ('postcoloniality') that the particular conditions that produced particular books can remain ignored, indeed even unavailable" (72–73).

Ultimately, the notion of a postcolonial literature which writes back to an undifferentiated colonial discourse leads to the kind of highly problematic, proscriptive categorization in which that literature is classified as deconstructive and carnivalesque in its opposition to monologic, authoritative colonial writing:

> The main difficulty with a warring dichotomy such as this is the limitations it imposes creating definitions which, no matter how focused on plurality, produce their own kind of orthodoxy. Thus, the postcolonial tends automatically to be thought of as multivocal, "mongrelized," and disruptive, even though this is not always the case. Similarly, on the other side of the binary, the

colonial need not always signify texts rigidly associated with the colonial power. Colonial, or even colonialist writing was never as invasively confident or as pompously dismissive of indigenous cultures as its oppositional pairing with postcolonial writing might suggest. (Boehmer 4)

As Elleke Boehmer's comments suggest, the writing back model posits a reductive unity not only among postcolonial literary texts but also among their Western intertexts. In the effort to place the "classics" in a colonial tradition, those ascribing to the writing back model reduce their significance to a collusion with colonial discourse. As a result, their particularity—including their often complex relationship with the colonial societies in which they were produced—is elided or, at least, made secondary.

The case of *Heart of Darkness* is particularly instructive in this regard since it is one of the central Western texts dealing with both Africa and colonialism. In his study of Europe's textual construction of Africa, Christopher Miller asserts *Heart of Darkness* is "the strongest of all Africanist texts"; it "reads as an allegory of all other Africanist texts; it defines the condition of possibility of Africanist discourse" (170).[9] Miller does not, however, see *Heart of Darkness* as representative of "European Africanist discourse"; like so many recent critics, he sees it as ambivalently positioned "between an old and a new mode of Africanist expression, between the projection of a corrupt and ignoble Africa and the later critique of that projection and its political outgrowth, colonialism" (171). As a result, Miller notes, recent literary criticism has struggled to categorize it: "it is neither colonialistic enough to be damnable nor ironic enough to be completely untainted by 'colonialist bias'" (171). In contrast with Miller, critics who apply the writing back model of reinscription characterize Conrad's novella as representative of a Western literary tradition which reproduced and legitimized Western colonial assumptions. A case in point: despite offering one of the most nuanced readings of *Heart of Darkness* in terms of its vision of colonialism, Said focuses primarily on the way Conrad "writes as a man whose *Western* view of the non-Western world is so ingrained as to blind him to other histories, other cultures, other aspirations" when he discusses the significance of African reinscriptions of Conrad's work (xviii).

A final problem with the writing back approach—one which has not received much critical attention—is that it severely limits the range of purposes and the transformative power of postcolonial reinscription of European literature. Because the postcolonial text is characterized as combating a colonial narrative, which the Western classic metonymically represents, the ultimate purpose of reinscribing the classic is to evoke and critique that narrative. Thus, the many intertextual relationships between European classics and postcolonial literatures are all defined in the same way—in terms of what Henry Louis Gates calls "motivated signifyin(g)." According to Gates, signifyin(g) "functions as a metaphor for formal revision, or intertextuality" (xxi); it is repetition with a difference. Unmotivated signifyin(g) or pastiche implies an act of homage; the revision is intended to indicate unity and resemblance. In contrast, motivated signifyin(g) or parody implies a negative critique and emphasizes difference (xxvii).[10] For those embracing the writing back approach, not only is the reinscription of Western classics by postcolonial literature always intended to enable critique but the critique itself always has the same purpose—to establish an anticolonial stance by countering the European classic and the colonial vision it represents.[11]

In an attempt to defend Conrad against accusations of racism and colonialism, some critics characterize the specific intertextual relationships between Conrad and African literature in terms of unmotivated signifyin(g). These critics claim the relationships are evidence African authors drew inspiration from an anticolonial spirit embedded in Conrad's fiction. For example, Peter Nazareth argues the appeal of Conrad for African writers rests on his being a "mental liberator" (221), while Andrea White asserts Conrad helped African authors develop their own attacks on colonialism and this influence proves his status as a profoundly anticolonial writer: "Several African writers I will discuss here seem to have recognized in Conrad, as an exoticized Other himself, some kindred understandings and concerns [. . .] they see Conrad as a kind of catalyst for refiguring the literary representation of the imperial endeavor and for deconstructing the myth of empire in a manner that created new possibilities for them as postcolonial writers" (198).[12] These critics obviously depart from the writing back approach in the sense that Conrad's fiction is now being aligned with postcolonial African literature in its focus on undermining the colonial narrative.[13] Nevertheless, they continue to employ the same conception of postcolonial literature which that approach entails, and African literature is still defined in terms of a focus on writing back to a singularly conceived, transhistorical colonial narrative. As is the case with the writing back approach, this results in a reductive simplification not only of African literature but also of the purposes of its reinscriptions of Conrad's fiction—the difference being Conrad's defenders represent all examples of reinscription as intended to establish

convergence and affiliation. In other words, if all postcolonial African fiction is writing back to the same colonial narrative as the one with which
Conrad was engaged, then however one categorizes Conrad's fiction in
terms of its relationship with that narrative (opposition or affiliation) will
determine how all the intertextual relationships between it and African
novels are to be defined.

The problem here is not necessarily that these approaches utilize the
colonial and the postcolonial as primary hermeneutic terms. Assuredly
colonialism has had a deep impact on African societies, and colonial relationships continue to operate throughout Africa in different forms in a
supposedly decolonized present. As a result, a good deal of African literature is focused on some form of colonialism and the need for decolonization. Like so many other -isms, however, colonialism is not a monolithic
entity; its form and ideology change as a result of numerous contextual
factors. Colonialism's heterogeneity is especially important to keep in
mind for the study of African fiction focused on the conditions leading
up to and resulting from the dissolution of the large, formal European
empires. This historical juncture sets up the most common literal meanings for colonialism and the postcolonial: the former signifying "the material condition of the political rule of subjugated peoples by the old European colonial powers" and the latter "an historical description of the
global political situation of a world of nominally independent sovereign
nation-states" (Young 27). However, the shift indicated by these definitions should not be taken to indicate transcendence. Among many
African authors, national independence and the problems facing the new
African nations resulted in an examination of how the specific constructions of those nations led to altered and different kinds of colonial domination. As a number of critics note, there are dangers in using the term
postcolonial if it implies "the demise of colonialism" (Loomba 7), since
such a use of the term can elide continued economic imperial relationships between the former colonizers and colonized and projects a problematic notion of progress which can be "prematurely celebratory"
(McClintock, "Angel" 294). Robert Young tries to take into consideration
such critical commentary when he defines the postcolonial as:

> coming after colonialism and imperialism, in their original mean-
> ing of direct-rule domination, but still positioned within imperi-
> alism in its later sense of the global system of hegemonic eco-
> nomic power. The postcolonial is a dialectical concept that marks
> the broad historical facts of decolonization and the determined

achievement of sovereignty—but also the realities of nations and
peoples emerging into a new imperialistic context of economic
and sometimes political domination. (57)

Yet, Young's definition does not entirely escape the kinds of problems
McClintock and Loomba detect in the suggestion of a movement beyond
colonialism suggested by the "post" in postcolonial. The problems with
this definition turn on the issue of the nation and its relationship with
colonialism. Young claims that the "post" refers to national liberation
from direct colonial rule but not freedom from other forms of imperialism. However, national independence did not necessarily result even in
freedom from direct colonial control for many within the new nations.
Discussing the way the new nation-states made "available the fruits of liberation only selectively and unevenly," Ania Loomba notes, "'Colonialism' is not just something that operates from outside a country or a people, not just something that operates with the collusion of forces inside,
but a version of it can be duplicated from within" (11–12). Young's definition only works if we focus on the relationship between newly independent nations and their former colonizers and repress forms of internal
colonization which occur "where the dominant part of a country treats a
group or region as it might a foreign colony" (McClintock, "Angel" 295).
To think of colonialism as operating only between nations is to ignore
some of its most insidious manifestations:

> Is South Africa "post-colonial"? East Timor? Australia? By what
> fiat of historical amnesia can the United States of America, in
> particular, qualify as "post-colonial"—a term which can only be
> a monumental affront to the Native American peoples currently
> opposing the confetti triumphalism of 1992? (McClintock,
> "Angel" 294)

Of course, forms of internal colonialism themselves vary enormously
depending, for example, on the interpenetration of European colonialism and local precolonial institutions, as well as the differences in forms
of European colonialism itself (British, French, Belgian, settler, non-set-
tler, etc.).[14]

Given these various forms of internal colonialism, the term postcolonial remains problematic if it is understood as marking a movement
beyond colonialism itself rather than a break from a particular kind of
colonialism. Even if one distinguishes between colonialism, defined as

direct rule, and imperialism, the question still remains: when and for whom has decolonization been achieved?[15] The equation between free-dom from European control and liberation from colonialism can all too easily encourage an exclusive focus on the struggle against external influ-ence and control and can, as a result, elide forms of internal national oppression. An issue confronted in the African novels in this study is pre-cisely how the struggle for liberation from new colonial and imperial structures and from forms of oppression that were de-emphasized by the fight for national independence brings into question conceptions of col-lective agency staged by European colonialism. These novels suggest the ambiguity of foundational political identities emphasized by recent post-colonial criticism and theory is not solely the product of postmodern influence, as some critics complain. Commenting on such critics (in par-ticular Arif Dirlik and Ella Shohat), Stuart Hall notes,

> A certain nostalgia runs through some of these arguments for a return to a clear-cut politics of binary oppositions, where clear "lines can be drawn in the sand" between goodies and bad-dies. [. . .] This is not as compelling an argument as it seems at first sight. These "lines" may have been simple once (were they?), but they certainly are so no longer. ("When Was 'The Post-Colo-nial'?" 244)

An important issue throughout this study is precisely how a complex con-fluence of historical and political factors—the shaping of the nation by colonialism, traditional forms of power, the operation of globalization, etc.—in post-independence African nations makes formulations of oppo-sitional identities based on single, uncomplicated categories (class, race, nationality, etc.) difficult and prevents political struggle from being sim-ple and clear.

It may be useful to define this perspective on collective identity with and against the theorizing of "Third-World" literature by Fredric Jame-son. Jameson claims there is a radical difference in consciousness between the West and its colonial others resulting from differences in modes of production—capitalist versus "so-called primitive" and "Asiatic" (68). In the West, Jameson argues, there is a radical split "between the private and the public, between the poetic and the political" while in "Third-World" cultures these binaries remain integrated (69). As a result, while political allegory is almost non-existent in "First World" literature, "all third-world texts are necessarily [. . .] allegorical and in a very specific way: they are to be read as what I will call *national allegories*" (69). As Aijaz Ahmed points out, however, the West (colonizer)/Rest (colonized) binary and the attendant focus on "Third-World" national allegory is the result of a focus on European colonialism and the nationalist struggles against it, and this approach comes at the expense of considering the heterogeneity of postcolonial nations both internally and in relation to one another:

> If societies [. . .] are defined not by relations of production but by relations of intra-national domination; if they are forever suspended outside the sphere of conflict between capitalism (First World) and socialism (Second World); if the motivating force for history here is neither class formation and class struggle nor the multiplicities of intersecting conflicts based upon class, gender, nation, race, region, and so on, but the unitary "experience" of national oppression . . . then what else *can* one narrate but that national oppression? (*In Theory* 102)

The approach to African novels in this study reinforces Ahmed's argument, emphasizing *how* these novels "narrate" forms of oppression and of collective identity other than those staged by a simplistic colonizer/colonized divide and how a focus on this idealist divide suppresses the complexity of conditions within nations.[16]

Jameson himself repeatedly brings into question his homogenizing of "Third-World" literature and the consciousness which produces it. He comments that

> the concept of cultural "identity" or even national "identity" is [not] adequate. One cannot acknowledge the justice of the general poststructuralist assault on the so-called "centered subject," the old unified ego of bourgeois individualism, and then resuscitate this same ideological mirage of psychic unification on the collective level in the form of a doctrine of collective identity. (78)

In turn, his reading of Ousmane Sembene's *Xala* works against such resuscitation. He discusses the novel in terms of class conflict within the postcolonial nation, and he claims "the deeper subject" of the novel is "the historical transformations of the traditional Islamic value of alms-giving in a contemporary money economy" (82). Such a reading focuses precisely on the fracturing of the categories of the nation and the "Third World"; the nation itself is riven by class rivalries which have complex relationships with extra-national economic forces, and consciousness within the postcolonial nation is formed by the intersection of capitalist ("Western") and pre-colonial institutions.

This literary reading would seem to open up the possibility of a different way of approaching "Third-World" literature, one focused both on the way that colonial binaries, which seemed to hold identity in place, are brought into question and on the search for different ways of theorizing identity and agency. Concomitantly, it seems to suggest political allegory in this literature is more varied than Jameson's initial theory suggested—that the collectivities being allegorized might be both below and above the nation.[17] My own readings of African fiction are in sync with this more complex historical materialist approach to "Third-World" literature, collective identity/consciousness, and political allegory. Unfortunately, in his conclusion, Jameson forecloses on the possibilities he offers by a return to the binary opposition of the West and the rest based on a colonial divide: "Hegel's old analysis of the Master-Slave relationship may still be the most effective way of dramatizing this distinction between two cultural logics" (85).

In contrast with Jameson's theorizing of their work, the African authors discussed in this study strive to represent politically effective conceptions of (non-oppressive) collective identity that will enable a continued struggle for decolonization in the face of the attenuation of the broad racial and cultural dichotomies encouraged by colonialism proper—black/white or Western/African. As a result, these authors will often reconstitute colonialism and decolonization (and the forms of agency they entail). These concepts are not immune from the historical condition of language, which, as Bakhtin insisted, is always in a "ceaseless flow of becoming" as a result of contextual usage:

> the word is not a material thing but rather the eternally mobile, eternally fickle medium of dialogic interaction. It never gravitates toward a single consciousness or a single voice. The life of the word is contained in its transfer from one mouth to another, from one context to another context, from one social collective to another, from one generation to another generation. In this process the word does not forget its own path and cannot completely free itself from the power of those concrete contexts into which it has entered. (201)

Bakhtin's observation is important for all the African novels discussed in this study, not only because meanings of colonialism and decolonization are transformed as result of their specific concerns and foci, but also because these novels insist on the importance of being attuned to such contextual transformation.

My focus on the dissemination of colonialism should not be taken as an endorsement of Aijaz Ahmed's claim that colonial discourse analysis, and postcolonial theory in general, is not pertinent to the study of most contemporary postcolonial literatures because it remains focused on older forms of colonialism. Ahmed complains that in "the cognate subdisciplines of 'Third World Literature' and 'Colonial Discourse Analysis'" there is "far greater interest in the colonialism of the past than in the imperialism of the present" (93). In contrast, my readings of African fiction support the notion that as a result of the deep and long-lasting impact of earlier forms of colonial discourse on newly independent nations, colonial discourse analysis is useful in understanding discursive conditions throughout contemporary Africa and in African fiction. A primary value of much postcolonial theory and scholarship is that it explores anew the attributes of nineteenth- and twentieth-century European colonialism and revisits the issue of how it lives on in a supposedly decolonized world. As Robert Young asserts, postcolonialism "involves a reconsideration of [the history of modern European colonization], particularly from the perspective of those who suffered its effects, together with the defining of its contemporary social and cultural impact. This is why postcolonial theory always intermingles the past with the present, why it is directed towards the active transformations of the present out of the clutches of the past" (4). What needs to be kept in mind is that trying to grasp "the contemporary and social impact" of European colonial history entails tracing the profound transformations and dissemination colonialism has undergone in a supposedly decolonized world.

For example, in *A Grain of Wheat,* Ngugi wa Thiong'o characterizes and targets a form of neocolonialism that arose in the wake of political independence. This characterization closely echoes Frantz Fanon's description of a postindependence condition in *The Wretched of the Earth,* in which he wrote of the exploitation of the supposedly decolonized nation by "native" elites working with Western capitalism[18]:

> Because [the native bourgeoisie] [. . .] lives to itself and cuts itself off from the people, undermined by its hereditary incapacity to think in terms of all the problems of the nation as seen from the point of view of the whole of that nation, the national middle

class will have nothing better to do than to take on the role of manager for Western enterprise, and it will in practice set up its country as the brothel of Europe. (154)

A Grain of Wheat emphasizes that, despite the links between them, there are important differences between the colonialism of the past and this new form of colonial control. Perhaps most important is the fact that certain equations dating from the period of nationalist liberation struggle break down. Colonialism can no longer be exclusively identified with white skin, and the end of direct European political control can no longer be equated with liberation. In fact, neocolonialism thrives on essentialist notions of race and place which suppress the importance of class as an analytic category and emphasize the idea that the enemy to be attacked is always white or foreign.[19] Speaking critically of African writing at the time of independence, Ngugi has pointed out,

> Except in a few cases, what was being celebrated in the writing was the departure of the whiteman with the implied hope that the incoming blackman by virtue of his blackness would right the wrongs and heal the wounds of centuries of slavery and colonialism. Were there classes in Africa? No! cried the nationalist politician, and the writer seemed to echo him. [. . .] As a result of this reductionism to the polarities of colour and race, the struggle of African people against European colonialism was seen in terms of a conflict of values between the African and the European ways of perceiving and reacting to reality. (63)

According to Ngugi, in the neocolony, holding onto a no longer relevant conception of colonialism, which constructs race and nation as primary forms of anticolonial agency, masks the operation of new forms of exploitation and undermines the struggle for liberation from reconstituted colonial structures. Similarly, an approach to *A Grain of Wheat* that overemphasizes the effort to write back to the colonizer—understood in racial and geographic terms—and that therefore obscures the importance of class as an analytic category, not only distorts the literary text but also prevents a thorough understanding of the operation of neocolonialism itself.

Tayeb Salih's *Season of Migration to the North* also focuses on the way a colonial epistemology based on racial and geographic oppositions (e.g., the British and the African, the modern and the traditional, the foreign

and the indigenous) is embraced by the formerly colonized and enables
neocolonialism to operate unopposed. Salih is particularly concerned
with how the traditional and indigenous are already transformed by the
deep impact of colonialism, as well as how remaining blind to this state
of affairs results in an unrecognized loss of self-determination and in the
perpetuation of both old and new forms of oppression. The novel
explores how a Manichean colonial epistemology has combined with a
traditional patriarchal culture to encourage the belief among the formerly
colonized that to "conquer" British women and to preserve traditional
oppressive gender roles constitute forms of anticolonial resistance. While
reinforcing traditional forms of gendered oppression, this rhetoric of
resistance masks the operation of neocolonialism by suggesting the imperial threat is always outside and foreign. Thus, Salih's novel reveals how
the transformation of precolonial local institutions by what Spivak refers
to as "the epistimic violence of colonialism" (76) becomes part of a specific kind of patriarchal neocolonial configuration in postindependence
Sudan, in part because the transformation itself is masked by the terms
imposed by that violence.

Reading African novels like *A Grain of Wheat,* and *Season of Migration to the North* in terms of their engagements with heterogenous colonial configurations has profound results for how their relationships with
Conradian intertexts are conceptualized. Because these configurations
are often significant departures from the forms of colonialism with
which Conrad was engaged, the purpose of reinscription is not necessarily defined by the effort to stake out an anticolonial position by being
aligned with a postcolonial vision or opposing a colonial narrative which
the Conradian intertext represents (depending on how one positions that
intertext). In other words, the link between the African novel and its
Conradian intertext is not determined by their respective relationships
with a common colonial narrative. Instead, in each case the significance
of the intertextual relationship depends on how the African novel makes
use of Conradian elements to construct and "write back" to its *specific*
configuration of the colonial and on how those elements are transformed
and given new meaning in the process. As a result, aspects of the Conradian intertexts other than those related to their positioning vis-à-vis colonialism can be of central importance in understanding and defining the
purpose of the reinscriptions. Just as important, when the intertext's relationship to colonialism is pertinent, its significance must be defined by
the historically specific concerns of the African novel. In other words,
even in this situation, the purpose of reinscription cannot necessarily be

reduced to an effort by the African author to be aligned with or opposed to Conrad's vision of colonialism. (As a result, there is not much concern in the following readings with categorizing the relationship between Conrad's fiction and the colonial narrative of his time in terms of collusion *or* critique, although there remains a consideration of the significance of his contradictory and complex perspective on colonialism for the various examples of intertextuality.) Ultimately, the absence of a defining common colonial narrative disrupts the clear-cut categorization of African/Conradian intertextuality in terms of motivated or unmotivated signifin(g); it results in a complex interweaving of convergence and divergence as the African novel uses the Conradian intertext to evoke conditions and perspectives that were beyond Conrad's historical knowledge or experience.

Chapter 1 explores how *No Longer At Ease*, Achebe's novel with the most explicit and extensive echoes of *Heart of Darkness*, employs this allusiveness not only to parody or counter the traditional colonial point of view Achebe (in "Image of Africa") reads as embedded in Conrad's novella, but also to reveal the dangers of a new kind of colonial fantasy among Nigerians. Specifically, *No Longer At Ease* reveals how conceptions of static and hierarchical identities undermine the egalitarian and adaptable perspective needed to *create* a productive national identity. Achebe represents Nigerians at the moment of independence as focused on the battle for power and spoils among towns, tribes, and classes (understood as immutable and unitary collectives). The ultimate result is a divided and corrupt incipient nation that threatens to perpetuate colonial economic relations with the metropolitan center and to produce new forms of internal colonialism. Achebe uses the Kurtz-like figure of Obi to represent this situation by emphasizing how a fantasy of polar, hierarchical identities has shaped him and how it leads to his downfall. Obi himself tries to use *Heart of Darkness* to define the transition from British colonial rule. However, thinking in terms of static and unitary identities, he remains unable to reflect on the transformations of identity wrought by colonial history which turn those like himself into the Kurtzes of a new colonial era. By setting up a contrast between his own and Obi's use of Conrad's novella, Achebe points to the dangers of Obi's sensibility, which remains blind to the transformative effects of history and to the necessity for an appropriately flexible approach to cultural forms. In this sense, *No Longer At Ease* not only exemplifies but also advocates for my approach to postcolonial intertextuality. In fact, a number of the critical principles applied in the following readings echo

Achebe's description of the Igbo aesthetic philosophy to which he sub-scribes. According to Achebe, the Igbo embrace a fluid, historically con-tingent vision of meaning and identity:

> In popular contemporary usage the Igbo formulate their view of the world as: "No condition is permanent." In Igbo cosmology even gods could fall out of use, and new forces are liable to appear without warning in the temporal and metaphysical firma-ment. (*Hopes* 64)

This philosophy results in a flexible and transformative aesthetic which mediates "between old and new, between accepted norms and extravagant aberrations" (*Hopes* 65).

Chapter 2 focuses on Ngugi wa Thiong'o's use of numerous ele-ments of plot, characterization, and theme from Conrad's *Under Western Eyes* in *A Grain of Wheat* in order to warn against neocolonialism and the long-term impact of colonial ideology in a newly liberated Kenya. In particular, many aspects of Conrad's novel work well to represent the threat of betrayal and disillusionment in the wake of independence. At the same time, Ngugi transforms the political significance of Conrad's narrative by altering its depictions not only of revolution but also of clearly delineated, essential national identities. In fact, Ngugi's use of *Under Western Eyes* represents a challenge to notions of national essences embedded in separate national cultures by making Conrad's novel part of an evolving Kenyan culture through the process of intertextual appro-priation and transformation.

In chapter 3, I argue that in *Season of Migration to The North,* Salih makes good use of the demythologizing aspects of Conrad's work in his exploration of how nationalist binaries enable unrecognized and uncharted forms of control to operate more effectively in postindepen-dence Sudan, resulting in the betrayal of oneself and others. Awareness of these aspects of Conrad's fiction contribute to a reader's understand-ing of the perspective offered by *Season of Migration to the North* on the Sudanese situation. At the same time, Salih transforms the Conradian elements by inserting them into a narrative focused on the sociohistori-cal origins of the problems faced by Sudan and on identifying founda-tions for a better, postcolonial future. Such a narrative is antithetical to Conrad's unremitting ironic vision of the human condition that erodes all foundations for constructing a better future and that leads to a kind of hopelessness—especially for the oppressed. Salih's process of appropriation and transformation enables him to make use of Conrad to evoke the ironic situation of a colonized postcolonial Sudan without subscribing to the hopeless malaise and corrosive skepticism Conrad's fiction so easily encourages.

The thesis of chapter 4 is that the intertextual relationship between *July's People* and *Heart of Darkness* is most interesting not as a means for Gordimer to challenge colonial discourse but in its implications for the deconstructive ambivalence of such discourse. On the one hand, both Gordimer's protagonist, Maureen Smales, and Conrad's narrator, Marlow, struggle to cling to their identities as their experiences in the African "wilderness" challenge their colonial assumptions and subjectivities. On the other hand, in *Heart of Darkness*, Marlow is able to continue to inhabit colonial roles because he travels up the Congo in the heyday of British imperialism, while *July's People* is precisely about what happens when such roles disintegrate in the context of the last gasp of direct European rule. Unlike Marlow, Maureen cannot recuperate her sense of authoritative identity; whenever she tries, the transformation of colonial relationships forces her to confront the constructed and contradictory nature of her subjectivity. In this sense, the intertextual relationship emphasizes that the disruptive potential in colonial discourse—as outlined in Homi Bhabha's early essays—can only be fully realized under specific social conditions; Gordimer posits a crucial link between the material instability of colonial roles and the lasting corrosion of colonial subjectivity. In *July's People* this more general point cannot be separated from Gordimer's historically specific warning that in the era of transition from white to black rule, white South Africans must change not just their ideas but their material practices if they are to become part of a new, progressive social order.[20]

Rather than examining the intertextual relationship between Ama Ata Aidoo's *Our Sister Killjoy* and *Heart of Darkness* primarily in terms of an effort to parody or reverse a European colonial vision as embedded in Conrad's novella (as other critics have done), chapter 5 explores the connection between this relationship and Aidoo's concerns with *new* forms of colonial control in a supposedly decolonized world. Echoing many arguments made by Frantz Fanon concerning national identity and culture, *Our Sister Killjoy* suggests a new, effective project of decolonization requires skepticism regarding the authoritative formulations of difference bequeathed by colonial and anticolonial rhetoric in the wake of national independence. By having her protagonist, Sissie, travel from Ghana to a Bavarian river town, Aidoo may reverse Marlow's journey from Europe to

Africa and set up Germany as a kind of heart of darkness. However, the relationship between the texts exceeds an easy colonial/postcolonial reading because both use similar narrative devices in order to reveal surreptitious connections between colonial and seemingly post- or anticolonial perspectives and disrupt the ideologically determined collective identities underpinning those perspectives.

By emphasizing the need to contextualize acts of writing and rewriting in precise historical terms, all of the following readings point to the limitations—even the dangers—in the analysis of African fiction of the static dialectic of colonial domination and postcolonial resistance underpinning the writing back approach to reinscription. These readings also bring into question both the standard literary binary (Western-colonial/African-postcolonial) this approach relies on and the concomitant focus on parodic intertextuality it encourages. Yet, these readings are neither based on notions of literary influence embraced by nativist and colonialist criticism nor do they support the representation of African/Conradian intertextuality as characterized by unifying convergence (unmotivated signifin[g]). Underpinned by the principles of Bakhtinian transformative revision, they counter restrictive and hierarchical assumptions on which most models of influence depend. At the same time, they undermine efforts to glorify Conrad using African appropriations of his work by emphasizing the divergences between the African novels and their Conradian intertexts. The following readings ultimately suggest a hybrid cultural production resulting from specific sociohistorical concerns in which acts of intertextual appropriation have purposes beyond opposition to or affiliation with the intertextual/intercultural literary other, and which result in shifting patterns of convergence, divergence, and transformation. This nexus of relations indicates the immense difficulty of defining how the processes of cultural hybridity and intertextuality operate, particularly in a postcolonial context.[21]

In *Culture and Imperialism,* Said argues that in the contemporary global situation, cultures have become interdependent and overlapping in part as a result of the history of twentieth-century imperialism: "Partly because of empire, all cultures are involved in one another; none is singular and pure, all are hybrid, heterogenous, extraordinarily differentiated, and unmonolithic" (xxv). Nevertheless, Said's analysis continues to lend itself to reading practices that limit the significance of this hybridity to a battle between different visions of colonialism—for example, in his claim that when "writers and scholars from the formerly colonized world have imposed their diverse histories on, have mapped their local geographies in, the great canonical texts of the European center," the significance of this reinscription is that it enables "new readings" of the "major metropolitan cultural texts" in terms of their complicity with empire (53). While the following readings reinforce Said's notion of overlapping cultures and his insistence on understanding the significance of cultural fusions in historical and political terms, they also suggest this significance need not be circumscribed by the notion of a debate between two opposed, conflictual visions of a particular kind of colonial relationship.

1

Extravagant Aberrations

Conrad, Hybridity, and
Chinua Achebe's *No Longer At Ease*

Chinua Achebe's literary relationship with Joseph Conrad would seem, on the face of it, to present one of the most straightforward cases of unambiguous postcolonial antagonism towards a colonial canon. In "Image of Africa," Achebe argues *Heart of Darkness* is "an offensive and deplorable book" which cannot "be called a great work of art" because it "depersonalizes a portion of the human race" (*Hopes* 12), and elsewhere he asserts it is part of the West's "monologue" on Africa which perpetuates racist myths: "I have no doubt that the reason for the high standing of *[Heart of Darkness]* is simply that it fortifies racial fears and prejudices" (*Hopes* 25). Achebe even claims his literary career was launched by a desire to counter the concept of Africa offered in *Heart of Darkness.* Yet, *No Longer At Ease,* Achebe's novel with the most explicit and extensive echoes of Conrad's novella, employs this allusiveness not simply or even primarily to parody or counter the traditional colonial point of view Achebe reads as embedded in *Heart of Darkness,* but to reveal the dangers of a new kind of colonial fantasy among Nigerians. In other words, Achebe's literary relationship with Conrad is more complex than his own statements suggest, since in at least one of his novels his invocation of *Heart of Darkness* is used for purposes other than writing back.

Representing *No Longer At Ease* as engaging in an explicitly combative relationship with *Heart of Darkness,* Philip Rogers asserts Achebe intends a "polemical parody of Conrad" (55). In this sense, his reading suggests *No Longer At Ease* is a literary precursor of "An Image of Africa."[1]

However, to claim Achebe appropriates aspects of *Heart of Darkness* solely or even primarily in order to attack Conrad is to ignore both the difference in historical moments of the novels and the primary concerns of *No Longer At Ease*. Achebe's novel is focused on the ideologies of identity among Nigerians resulting from the subtle effects of both the colonialism of Conrad's day and post-World War II colonial policy. These ideologies have resulted in a divided, chaotic, and corrupt incipient nation which threatens to perpetuate colonial economic relations with the metropolitan center and to produce new forms of internal colonialism. In other words, *No Longer At Ease* suggests the "heart of darkness" is a new colonial mindset, which has developed among Nigerians and which is antithetical to the development of a strong and unified postcolonial nation. Rogers' argument that Achebe "parodies" Conrad results in eliding the complexity of this condition, and leads to a distortion of the novel. The oppositional relationship implied in the notion of parody encourages Rogers to read *No Longer At Ease* as reversing the valuation of the binary terms of *Heart of Darkness* (white/black, European/African); he claims Achebe ascribes "to whiteness and light the deadly qualities Conrad gave to darkness"(56) and the problems in *No Longer At Ease* are caused by the Europeanized Obi Okonkwo's "hollow heart of . . . whiteness" (54). In opposition to this deadly "whiteness" is "black fertility and sexuality" (58) and "the core of enduring, if threatened, African values and vitality" (55). However, the hierarchical dichotomy Rogers posits reproduces the kind of Manichean fantasy which in *No Longer At Ease* contributes to neocolonial perspectives among all segments of Nigeria. These perspectives not only created a degraded society but also undermined the historical and adaptable perspective needed to create a truly postcolonial Nigerian consciousness.

In order to represent this situation, Achebe uses Conrad's Kurtz as a kind of model for his antihero Obi. Both Kurtz and Obi organize the world using the hierarchical polarities of romance (light/dark, good/evil), which enable them to think of themselves as transcendent, heroic figures separated from the evil they seek to combat. As a result, they are blind to the actual nature of the darkness (as constituted differently by each text) and to its presence in themselves when they travel from Europe to Africa on their quest to save Africa or, in Obi's case, Nigeria. Their romantic vision is summed up in *No Longer At Ease* through a direct quotation from Kurtz's report to the International Society for the Suppression of Savage Customs: "By the simple exercise of our will we can exert a power for good practically unbounded" (121). Blind to their real conditions of existence, not only are Obi and Kurtz unsuccessful in their efforts to improve conditions in Africa, but they themselves ultimately degenerate and come to embody the forces against which they define themselves.

In *No Longer At Ease,* the dangerous fantasies of identity the novel attacks are the legacy of shifting colonial ideology and policies. Achebe represents British imperialism as having initially given Europeans an absolute, godlike authority over colonized peoples, which was legitimated by notions of essentialized and hierarchically organized racial and cultural identities. The character of Mr. Green, stereotypic of the old style colonial British man, reflects the kind of mentality this situation produced. Green "loved Africa, but only Africa of a kind: the Africa of Charles the messenger, the Africa of his gardenboy and steward boy" (121). Although he is devoted to his "duty" to "civilize" Nigeria, he does not believe or want to believe that Africans can really be improved; civilization requires the permanent guidance and control of Europeans. However, *No Longer At Ease* depicts Green's conception of colonial authority and his corresponding conception of identity as outdated. The change in roles and attitudes among the British is suggested by the story of a British "Inspector of Schools" from Obi's youth who, in the midst of an inspection, tells a headmaster to "Shut up!" and slaps him. The headmaster instinctively throws him on the ground: "Without knowing why, teachers and pupils all took to their heels. To throw a white man was like unmasking an ancestral spirit" (74). "Twenty years" later things have changed: "Today few white men would dream of slapping a headmaster in his school and none at all would actually do it" (74). This transformation results from specific changes in colonial policy. After World War II, the British realized that they would need to change their approach to make the colonies more productive (Freund 170). The resulting "new deal" for Africa was the administrative foundation of neocolonialism (although the British had no intention in the late 1940s of decolonizing in the next 20 years). One aspect of this new deal was an active and organized increase in the level of collaboration between the British and an African nationalist educated elite (Freund 176). Increasingly, these elites were given positions and privileges formerly reserved for Europeans. The result was the development of a Europeanized African ruling stratum that would eventually take over the colonial state hierarchy and protect the interests of the colonizers (Freund 210–11).

In *No Longer At Ease,* these circumstances create a situation in which, on the one hand, Nigerians can aspire to the status of the colonizer and, on the other, the only way to achieve this status is through a British education. The colonial fantasy of a transcendent, collective identity with its attendant rigidly hierarchical political and social structure is not done away with but is reformulated in terms which encourage that fantasy among the colonized. Nigerians are now focused on attaining the mystical power of the colonizer through an equally mystical education. The goal is to establish one's group as the replacement for the colonizers both ontologically and politically—to be defined as both separate from and superior to the majority of Nigerians—rather than to get rid of the colonial hierarchy or the underlying conception of identity on which it was based.

In *No Longer At Ease,* the colonial fantasy of transcendence, as embraced by Nigerians, has had catastrophic effects: it hampers the development of principles which are crucial for building a strong, unified postcolonial nation and results in a divided and corrupt society. Because an undefined spiritual immanence conferred by British education and, more generally, the trappings of British identity have come to represent the pinnacle of progress, practical means of measuring success and progress are undermined by mystical colonial fetishism. At the same time, Nigerians embrace a fantasy of static, unified collective identities and are blind to the actual historical and fluid nature of these identities. As a result, they are unable to reflect on how colonial history has shaped the social landscape—encouraging divisions but also creating new couplings—and they cannot respond to the effects of that history adequately by forging a new and appropriate community. In particular, Nigerians are unable to create a national identity and a corresponding sense of national responsibility which would effectively enable them to address their new (social) conditions and build a better future. Instead, they focus on the battle for power and spoils among different groups within Nigeria. The ultimate effect of the colonial fantasy among all segments of Nigeria is a degraded present and lack of constructive grounding for the future. As Abdul JanMohamed points out, the incipient nation is "a society paralyzed by corruption, cynicism towards the colonial government, confusion about old and new values, a lack of social coherence, and an absence of historical direction" (182).

However, *No Longer At Ease* is not an entirely pessimistic novel; in the proverbs and rituals of the Umuofians one finds the vestiges of values that could lay the foundation for a better future. For example, many of the Umuofians' proverbs emphasize the importance of reliance on communal interdependence and strength for protection and empowerment: "'Our fathers also have a saying about the danger of living apart. They say it is the curse of the snake. If all snakes lived together in one place, who would approach them? But they live every one unto himself and so fall easy prey to man'" (92–93). This proverb—if applied to the nation—would suggest a strong Nigeria could be achieved if individuals and groups think of themselves as parts of a larger community which must work with each other and rely on the strength of the community itself to cope with external threats (such as the predatory practices of neocolonialism), rather than remaining focused on individual or narrow group interests or relying on the transcendence of those with British educations. However, this form of nationalism necessitates a willingness and ability to widen the concept of the interdependent community to include the nation as a whole.

In his essays, Achebe suggests that in Igbo philosophy identity is contingent; it can and needs to be altered as a result of historical circumstances. He claims, for example, that the Igbo ensure the survival and prosperity of the community by countering a shifting reality with a fluid culture:

> In popular contemporary usage the Igbo formulate their view of the world as: "No condition is permanent." In Igbo cosmology even gods could fall out of use, and new forces are liable to appear without warning in the temporal and metaphysical firmament. The practical purpose of art is to channel a spiritual force into an aesthetically satisfying physical form that captures the presumed attributes of that force. It stands to reason, therefore, that new forms must stand ready to be called into being as often as new (threatening) forces appear on the scene. It is like "earthing" an electrical charge to ensure communal safety. (*Hopes* 64)

In *No Longer At Ease,* this adaptive approach and its benefits are revealed when an Igbo village elder, Ogubuefi Odogwu, creates a new cultural tradition in the face of the potentially divisive conditions brought about by colonialism. Although he is not Christian, he blends the ceremony of the breaking of the kola with the language of Christianity in order both to celebrate Obi's homecoming in a traditional manner and to satisfy Obi's father—who as a Christian does not approve of "pagan" ceremonies. Ogubuefi's fellow Umuofians display an appreciation of this constructive and flexible approach to the situation: "Everyone replied Amen and cheered old Odogwu on his performance" (60). As this situation suggests, in Achebe's fiction it is clear such adaptability must be applied to the concepts of community to which aesthetic and spiritual forms are inextricably tied. For example, in *Arrow of God,* the attacks of a neighboring clan lead six villages to join forces and form both Umuaro, a new political and social entity, and Ulu, a god for Umuaro: "From that day they were never again beaten by an enemy" (15).

If hope for the future in *No Longer At Ease* is to be found in the same Igbo principles that led to the empowerment of Umuaro in *Arrow of God*, the deep pessimism of the novel lies partly in the way these principles have been yoked with neocolonial values by the Umuofians. This is particularly obvious in their approach to colonial education. Apparently ascribing to the principle of the interdependent community, they sacrificed a great deal to send Obi to England because they believed that simply by having a "kinsman" with a British education they would progress. As a result, when he returns they view him as a hero who has acquired the means of saving them. Despite his youth, he has become one of the elders of the clan. Thus, he is given on his return "a royal welcome" by the Umuofian Union, and is compared in the Union's Secretary's speech to Jason back with "the Golden Fleece" (35–36). The mythical and abstract language of the speech indicates Obi and his education are valorized solely because of their connection with the mystical power of the colonizer, not because of any concrete skills, knowledge, or character traits they reflect. The Umuofians have put their faith for the future in a boy simply because he has become more closely identified with the colonizer, and they have lost faith in the power of the community as a whole.

Ironically, the Umuofians' conception of community and communal interest is itself evidence of the impact of colonialism; the focus on competition for British status has significantly contributed to an inflexible approach to collective identity. For example, after Obi is caught for bribery, the Umuofians despair because they see themselves as losing a competition with other villages for the spoils of independence. Nigeria does not represent a possible manifestation of a new kind of community, only a battleground for already existing social groups: "'Many towns have four or five or even ten of their sons in European posts in this city [Lagos]. Umuofia has only one. And now our enemies say that even that one is too many for us" (7). Focused on this competition, the Umuofians are unable to think flexibly about collective identity and to entertain the possibility of a new national community; as a result, "towns all over Nigeria" can only be foreign lands to which they travel "to find work" but in which they remain "sojourners." (5). At an Umuofian Union meeting in Lagos, the capital of the future Nigeria, one of the elders says: "We are strangers in this land. If good comes to it may we have our share. [. . .] But if bad comes let it go to the owners of the land who know what gods should be appeased" (7). When Obi tries to suggest to the Umuofian Union, made up of those Umuofians who work in Lagos, that there is a need to focus on national service as opposed to individual or narrow group interest, they disapprove of his speech because "In Nigeria the government was 'they.' It had nothing to do with you or me. It was an alien institution and people's business was to get as much from it as they could without getting into trouble" (37).² Such an attitude has been overdetermined by colonialism since it not only encouraged ossification and division among communities in Nigeria, but also resulted in an autocratic administration which alienated the people. The lack of a sense of national identity or responsibility to a national government contributes to the ubiquitous corruption since there is no sense of a national community to which one has ethical responsibilities.

Achebe suggests the notion of a unitary Umuofia is a fantasy by referring to the many divisions among different Umuofian groups; these internal divisions serve to highlight the fluidity of communal identity and interest. Religion, in particular, is a cause of fragmentation. When Obi returns for a visit to Umuofia, his school's band "played an old evangelical turn which in Obi's schooldays Protestant schoolchildren had sung to anti-Catholic words, especially on Empire Day, when Protestants and Catholics competed in athletics" (57). Even more severe is the antagonism between the uncompromising Christians like Obi's father and those who still hold animist beliefs and who at one time were called "the people of nothing" by the Christians (66). These conflicts among religious groups in Umuofia suggest not only the plural nature of an Umuofian identity but also the danger of not acknowledging its plurality and contingency. To accept a myth of an objective, single Umuofia ignores the need for the kind of constructive work done by Odogwu when he appeases both Obi's father and the animists through a hybrid welcoming ceremony for Obi. The result can only be a further fracturing of a sense of community.

The ironic link between the Umuofians' unreflecting myth of collective identity and communal division is reflected in their attitude towards Obi. The Umuofians believe if they send Obi off for a British education, he will necessarily remain tied to the community. As a result, they remain blind to the potential divisive effects of that education—reflected in Obi's own representation of the significance of his degree—which include both a new sense of class-based group identity and increased individualism:

> A university degree was the philosopher's stone. It transmuted a third-class clerk on one hundred and fifty a year into a senior civil

servant on five hundred and seventy, with car and luxuriously
furnished quarters at nominal rent. And the disparity in salary
and amenities did not tell even half the story. To occupy a "European post" was second only to actually being a European. It
raised a man from the masses to the elite whose small talk at
cocktail parties was: "How's the car behaving?" (105)

A university education is conceived solely in terms of the transformation
and elevation of individuals, not of a community. At the same time, that a
university degree is important because it raises "a man from the masses to
the elite" suggests the development of a new class of Nigerians who consider themselves above the rest of the nation. This new class believes in its
natural right to the status and privilege of the colonizer because of its cultural and intellectual connection with the British. Believing in the myths
both of Umuofian identity and of the transcendence conferred by a colonial education, the Umuofians unwittingly contribute to division within
their own community and, more generally, to a divisive force in Nigeria as
a whole—a new *class* embracing colonial elitism and individualism.[3]

In one sense, it appears that Obi, rather than embodying a danger for
the future, represents a hope for national unity in that he embraces the
notion of a Nigerian community. A speech he makes to the Union on his
return suggests this sense of hope: "Education for service, not for white-
collar jobs and comfortable salaries. With our great country on the
threshold of independence, we need men who are prepared to serve her
well and truly" (37). However, the problem is that, as Obi's patriotic language suggests ("our great country"), he does not recognize that a sense of
Nigerian identity is not something given but something that must be
made. Obi assumes "that Nigeria is a stable and knowable community,
even when the narrative (and his own experience) call attention to the
unformed character of the national community. Clearly, Obi's Nigeria is
a fantasy which the narrative challenges along the way" (Gikandi, *Achebe*
86).[4] As Simon Gikandi suggests, Obi's Nigeria is another fantasy of community spawned by colonial discourse. Separated from their original
communities by education and their subsequent entry into a new class,
the elites turn to the notion of the nation in order to imagine a sense of
place and belonging.[5] Only when he is in England and separated from the
reality of Nigeria, for example, does Obi begin to think in terms of a
Nigerian identity: "in England [. . .] Nigeria first became more than just
a name to him. That was the first great thing that England did for him"
(14). In fact, the Nigeria Obi embraces is a nationalist romance, its form

spawned by the desire for a transcendent, ideal identity that would reverse the fantasy of Africa posited by colonial ideology. This ideal identity is reflected in the poetry Obi writes while in England:

> God bless our noble fatherland
> Great land of sunshine bright,
> Where brave men chose the way of peace,
> To win their freedom fight.
> May we preserve our purity,
> Our zest for life and jollity. (118)

Obi's clichéd images project a Nigerian essence defined by a "purity" and "zest for life and jollity." He ignores the fact that Nigeria in its current state *is* a result of the historical processes of colonialism—there is no purity to be preserved.[6]

Even when he is confronted by a real problem resulting from the historical construction of Nigeria, Obi can only think about it in terms of a European nationalist ideology which assumes the existence of national essences and which posits a hierarchy of nations based on them: "when [Obi] had to speak in English with a Nigerian student from another tribe he lowered his voice. It was humiliating to have to speak to one's countrymen in a foreign language, especially in the presence of the proud owners of that language. They would naturally assume that one had no language of one's own" (57). Obsessed with the issue of status and assuming a link between national essences and national languages, Obi only thinks of his embarrassment when faced with Nigeria's lack of a non-European national language; he is unable to reflect on the fact that Nigeria's only common language is English because it has been constructed by colonialism. This makes it impossible for him to think about the extremely difficult problem of a national language in practical and constructive terms. Focused on laying claim to an already existing, primordial national identity of which he can be proud, Obi cannot grasp the difficult cultural work necessitated by the historical conditions of Nigeria's development.

Of course, even while in England, Obi is not blind to Nigeria's divided, corrupt, and psychically colonized condition, but he simply believes the rest of the nation needs to follow the lead of the educated elite, like himself, who have been able to overcome a colonial mentality and access a pure, transcendent Nigerian spirit free from taint. When Obi gets back to Nigeria and is overwhelmed by the conditions he finds, he does not abandon his nationalist fantasy but simply thinks of his class as encompassing the "real" Nigeria. By the time Obi takes his first trip home to Umuofia, the combination of his horror at the corruption in Nigeria and his vision of his class's strong moral fiber leads him to assume a natural, unbridgeable difference between the educated elite and the rest of Nigeria. This assumption, in turn, results in a conception of Nigeria along strictly colonial lines, with the educated elites replacing the colonizers and representing the ideal nation:

> What an Augean stable! [. . .] Where does one begin? With the masses? Educate the masses? [. . .] Not a chance there. It would take centuries. A handful of men at the top. Or even one man with vision—an enlightened dictator. People are scared of the word nowadays. But what kind of democracy can exist side by side with so much corruption and ignorance? [. . .] (50–51)

Obi concludes Nigeria's corruption is the result of the natural developmental level of the masses which makes education useless for them. Beneath this explanation lies the assumption that the educated elite, from which the "handful of men at the top" would come, are superior not just because of their education but also because they have the natural capacity to be effectively enlightened. As a result of this assumption, Obi can only envision an authoritarian, colonialist government for Nigeria after independence, which will strictly control the masses, who, like children, cannot govern themselves. The horrible irony of Obi's condemnation of the masses is that while he sees them living in a darkness from which the "enlightened dictator" would save them, in the context of the novel the actual darkness is the unrecognized control exerted by colonial ideology over all Nigerians, elite and masses alike, which will result in a neocolonial state ruled by "a handful of men at the top." This irony links Obi directly with Conrad's Kurtz in that both believe they have transcended the darkness because of the inherent nature of a group to which they belong; this belief blinds them to the presence of the darkness in themselves and causes them to facilitate its operation.

Obi represents the threat of a neocolonial future not only because he conceives of the internal structure of the future nation in colonial terms, but also because his elitism results in unreflecting consumption of Western commodities which ultimately does him no good and contributes enormously to his severe financial problems. When Obi reflects that what raises "a man from the masses to the elite" (what makes him "second only to actually being a European") is his ability to engage in small talk

("How's the car behaving"), he reveals the importance of owning expensive consumer goods which are signs of membership in that elite. In *No Longer At Ease,* this situation results in a vast expenditure of resources on these goods. When Obi begins working for the civil service he purchases a new car on credit and overextends himself financially on its upkeep and insurance; the car, then, is a major source of his severe economic problems. Obi's reason for keeping it, despite these problems, is emphasized when he rationalizes his inability to pay off his debt to the Umuofia Progressive Union:

> Having labored in sweat and tears to enroll their kinsman among the shining elite, [the Umuofians] had to keep him there. Having made him a member of an exclusive club whose members greeted one another with "How's the car behaving?" did they expect him to turn round and answer: "I'm sorry, but my car is off the road. You see I couldn't pay my insurance premium?" That would be letting the side down in a way that was quite unthinkable. Almost as unthinkable as a masked spirit in the old Ibo society answering another's esoteric salutation: "I'm sorry, my friend, but I don't understand your strange language. I'm but a human being wearing a mask." No these things could not be. (113)

Despite all the problems it causes him (and the Union), Obi keeps and maintains the car not primarily for the benefits its use provides, but in order to mark his inclusion in an exclusive class—"the shining elite"— who have transcended the condition of mere mortal Nigerians and attained a godlike European status.

The real beneficiaries of this consumption are the British. The most expensive consumer goods—such as Obi's car, which is a British-made "Morris Oxford"—are imported from Britain, and their purchase contributes little to the development of Nigeria's economy or infrastructure, while using up much needed financial capital (just as Obi's ownership of the car offers him few practical benefits while propelling him into serious financial difficulties). To some degree this situation reflects the historical reality of Nigeria and Britain's economic relationship in the 1950s; the confluence of two of Britain's policies for a post-World War II "New Deal" for Africa—the increase in the importation of expensive consumer goods and the effort to create a small relatively wealthy class of Africans with whom the British could collaborate—resulted in the increase of the purchase of expensive consumer goods made in Europe. Because the new deal involved the manufacturing of cheaper mass consumption goods locally,

> the profile of the [dominant export-import houses'] interests changed rapidly as the "second colonial occupation" shifted the import cargoes increasingly from basic industrial consumer goods to machinery and capital goods. The import, marketing and servicing of automobiles became big business. Firms such as the United Africa Company withdrew from produce storage in small market canteen centres to concentrate on establishing retail department stores in the major cities. (Freund 171–172)

Given the fact that cars and goods sold in department stores would obviously be too expensive for most Africans, the focus of the new import policy was on a small, primarily urban, wage-earning group in the industrial, business, and civil service sectors. The most expensive of these goods, such as cars, would only be available to the most privileged of Africans. In this situation, the elitism encouraged by the new colonial policies would be a powerful means of marketing these goods as status symbols.

Eventually, Obi's financial problems lead him to take bribes, and the link between these problems and his elitism suggests one way in which conceptions of identity bequeathed by colonialism result in Nigeria's corrupt condition. Equally important, in this regard is that Obi's elitist fantasy results in a lack of any grounded, practical principles which could provide the resolve to resist taking bribes. As C.L. Innes points out, Obi "has no consistent set of values or convictions on which to stand firm" beside "the belief in individual fulfilment and romance" (Innes, *Achebe* 55). Obi himself becomes aware of this lack of conviction when he tries to convince his parents to accept his engagement to Clara—who as an Osu is considered an outcast. His inability to find any convincing arguments, combined with his mother and father's adamant opposition to the idea of his marriage, forces him to a partial epiphany:

> His mind was troubled not only by what had happened but also by the discovery that there was nothing in him with which to challenge it honestly. All day he had striven to rouse his anger and his conviction, but he was honest enough with himself to realize that the response he got, no matter how violent it some-

times appeared, was not genuine. It came from the periphery, and not the center, like the jerk in the leg of a dead frog when a current is applied to it. (156)

This moment when Obi looks into himself and finds a hollowness suggests another link with Kurtz. Marlow claims Kurtz "was hollow at the core": "there was something wanting in him—some small matter which when the pressing need arose could not be found under his magnificent eloquence" (57–58). Focused on their own exalted conceptions of themselves, Obi and Kurtz do not develop grounded convictions based on something other than their colonial heroic romances. In both cases, the result is a hollow man without restraints. Marlow complains of Kurtz: "I had to deal with a being to whom I could not appeal in the name of anything high or low. I had [. . .] to invoke him—himself—his own exalted and incredible degradation. There was nothing either above or below him. [. . .] He had kicked himself loose of the earth. Confound the man! He had kicked the very earth to pieces" (65). An important difference between the two characters, nevertheless, is that while Marlow suggests Kurtz comes to a full understanding of his life and is able to pronounce judgment on it ("the horror"), there is no corresponding suggestion about Obi in *No Longer At Ease*. Instead of delving deeper into the implications of his epiphany, Obi avoids reflecting on it and literally runs back to Lagos where his scruples about taking bribes are easily overcome once his financial problems become overwhelming.

Obi's lack of any true understanding of his condition throughout the course of the narrative should come as no surprise to the careful reader. In the scene of his trial for corruption, with which the novel begins, he remains completely and unwittingly controlled by his neocolonial romance. Entering into the courtroom, he "appeared unruffled and indifferent. The proceeding seemed to be of little interest to him" (1). In the midst of the trial, however, this pose briefly breaks down: "It was only when [the judge] said: 'I cannot comprehend how a young man of your education and brilliant promise could have done this' that a sudden and marked change occurred. Treacherous tears came into Obi's eyes" (2). Obi has never understood or come to grips with his elitist fantasy and so he cannot control his reactions when the judge refers to the foundation of his belief in his superiority—his "education and brilliant promise." Even after this breakdown, in his last thoughts at the trial, Obi does not reflect on why he cried and can only regret his loss of composure: "now when the supreme moment came he was betrayed by treacherous tears" (3).

Obi's last chronological moment (but first narrative appearance) in the novel, therefore, serves to stress his unperceived and unrelieved colonized condition. As a result, the first scene foregrounds the novel's subversion of two notions of promise. First, *No Longer At Ease* unravels the destiny equated with a British education. As Gikandi asserts, "Achebe's plot deliberately subverts the logic of promise and destiny which underlies Obi's quest" (92). Second, Achebe frustrates the promise of the tragic hero's enlightenment. In this sense, Achebe's novel is both like and unlike *Heart of Darkness,* which might undo the destiny traditionally associated with the colonial hero (Kurtz) but which still gives that figure the appearance of an heroic epiphany.

Given the fact Obi is an absolutely controlled and unenlightened protagonist, Achebe's focus in *No Longer At Ease* is clearly not on the tragedy of the fall of an exceptional individual. However, there is a tragedy here: the hope of a postcolonial Nigeria is destroyed by the fatal flaw of a neocolonial fantasy of identity. Obi epitomizes this flaw but he does not encompass it. C.L. Innes concludes her reading of *No Longer At Ease* with the claim that "For Achebe, [. . .] young been-tos' like Obi who adopt the 'fashionable pessimism' of the West are the problem" (63); this claim is in line with her reading of the novel which, like many other critics', elides the fact that the "young been-tos'" of Achebe's novel are in many ways the result of the widespread colonization of all segments of Nigerian society and culture. If Obi and the class of Nigerians to which he belongs are the culmination of the destructive effects of colonial policy and ideology, Achebe makes it clear that, just as all of Europe contributed to the making of Kurtz, all of Nigeria—including traditional communities such as Umuofia—contributed to the making of Obi and his class.

In *No Longer At Ease,* the full horror of Nigeria's condition is reflected by the lack of understanding in any character of colonialism's legacy—a lack which is at the center of the novel's narrative structure. Since, from the first page, the reader knows the outcome of Obi's story, the focus of the narrative is on the causes of his situation. This focus is also signaled in the first chapter by Mr. Green's attempt to explain these causes: "The fact that over countless centuries the African has been the victim of the worst climate in the world and of every imaginable disease. Hardly his fault. But he has been sapped mentally and physically" (4). The rest of the novel reveals the absurdity and inadequacy of Green's racist reasoning. As a result, *No Longer At Ease* foregrounds its warning against causal analysis based on homogenous, natural conceptions of group identity, even as it points to the link between such conceptions and colonial ideology. Thus, when Union members try to explain Obi by turning to the notion of family bloodlines—"A man may go to England, become a lawyer or a doctor, but it does not change his blood" (182)—such reductive reasoning based on the notion of blood has already been discredited. Significantly, both Green and the Union shift responsibility away from themselves, much as Obi's own elitist fantasy enables him to avoid implicating himself in Nigeria's condition. The ending of the novel emphasizes the resulting lack of enlightenment:

> Everybody wondered why. The learned judge, as we have seen, could not comprehend how an educated young man and so on and so forth. The British Council man, even the men of Umuofia, did not know. And we must presume that, in spite of his certitude, Mr. Green did not know either. (194)

The fact that no character in the novel understands Obi's condition suggests Nigeria is in grave danger, since without an understanding of the complex effects of colonial policy and ideology the promise of a postcolonial future will be aborted (just like Clara and Obi's child). Hope is built into the novel to the degree readers are able to look closely at Obi's story, avoid reductive explanations like Green's and the Umuofians', and recognize how colonial rule has organized the Nigerian psyche.[7]

The link between the narrative structure of *No Longer At Ease* and the issue of enlightenment suggests another connection between Achebe's novel and *Heart of Darkness*. The narrative frame of Conrad's novel also emphasizes the search for meaning in past events, since it focuses attention on Marlow's effort through storytelling both to gain insight into his experiences and to unsettle his listeners—at least one of whom (Conrad's first narrator) thinks as simplistically as the characters trying to figure out Obi's plight in *No Longer At Ease*. However, if the focus on enlightenment is similar, its content is different. *Heart of Darkness* encourages a search for a timeless, universal, and dark truth embodied by "the horror," although the exact nature of this truth remains up for hermeneutic grabs. (It could, of course, be the paradoxical impossibility of arriving at any truth—as J. Hillis Miller puts it, the "enlightenment [. . .] is of the fact that the darkness can never be enlightened" [48]—although, even in this case, it would still embody a kind of perennial human condition.) In contrast, *No Longer At Ease* focuses attention on the historical nature of the distressing truth. In this case the "horror" stems from specific political and socio-economic causes. As a result, Achebe's novel is ultimately less pessimistic than

Conrad's because it suggests the darkness is something that could be overcome. In fact, the hope for the future in *No Longer At Ease*—embracing a
historically oriented philosophical vision—is in direct conflict with the
notion of the fatalistic timeless truths embedded in *Heart of Darkness*. In
one sense, it *is* strange to assert Achebe's novel is more optimistic than
Conrad's because the lack of actual enlightenment by any character offers
a pessimistic perspective on Nigeria's immediate future. Only in an
enlightened critical readership is there the hope of combating the colonialist darkness.[8]

Achebe's transformatory application of British literature—his appropriation of Conrad's text for a new set of concerns—contrasts vividly
with Obi's own use of that literature. Obi's training in English literature
is useless in terms of addressing Nigeria's problems because of his
Manichean romanticism. This is revealed when he ponders the applica-
bility of *Heart of Darkness* to Green's situation: "It was not a close anal-
ogy, of course. Kurtz had succumbed to the darkness, Green to the incipient dawn. But their beginning and their end were alike. I must write a
novel on the tragedy of the Greens of this century, [Obi] thought,
pleased with his analysis" (121–122). Unable to perceive how historical
transformations of colonialism render his clear-cut dichotomies absurd,
Obi suggests an easy split between the darkness of the colonial past and
"the incipient dawn" of independence. He also makes an absolute distinction between the old-style colonial white men—Kurtz and Green—
and himself, a member of the new, African "shining elite" leading the
way into the light. In other words, Obi can neither think about colonialism as something which could continue into the postindependence
future in a new guise—it can only be understood by him in terms of
direct British rule—nor contemplate new meanings for Conrad's Kurtz
resulting from the transformation of identities. In contrast, *No Longer At
Ease* represents the problems resulting from new manifestations of colonialism, and it uses aspects of Conrad's novel to do so. Instead of writing a book focused on the tragedy of the Greens, Achebe has written a
book focused on the tragedy of the Obis—that is, the tragedy of a neocolonial present reflected in a *Nigerian* Kurtz. By transforming a fictional
character produced in a particular set of historical circumstances, in
order to address a very different set of historical concerns, Achebe
remains true to an Igbo aesthetic philosophy (or, at least, his version of
that philosophy) rooted in a historical and practical consciousness and
resulting in an art that mediates "between old and new, between
accepted norms and extravagant aberrations" (*Hopes* 65).[9]

The link between the transformatory aspect of Achebe's textual practice and his discussion of Igbo aesthetics points to the way in which an apparently nostalgic nativist nationalism in his work—a desire to found a future Nigeria on Igbo culture—is in actuality an important part of his project to construct a hybrid Nigerian consciousness. In *No Longer At Ease,* hope for a postcolonial future is to be found in part in a historical and flexible Igbo philosophy which embraces hybridity and challenges notions of fixed collective essences embedded in both colonial ideology and nativism. *No Longer At Ease* can be considered a good example of this philosophy put into aesthetic practice. Achebe's stylistic hybridity, in which he melds an Igbo oral tradition with the novel form, ultimately defies any attempt to hierarchize or even separate the two traditions. If the Igbo proverbs explicitly articulate values which ground the postcolonial future, it is the articulation of those proverbs within the distinctly Conradian narrative which reveals the need to apply those values to the specific historical circumstances of Nigeria in the late 1950s. In this sense, the novel advocates an awareness of and ability to manipulate the inextricable blendings of cultures and traditions that are an inevitable result of history.

In his essay, "Named for Victoria, Queen of England," Achebe explicitly claims that hope for the postcolonial nation lies, ironically, in the hybridity created by colonialism itself. He uses the metaphor of "the crossroads" to describe the intersection of two cultures, but the metaphor emphasizes that at this place it is impossible to extricate them; they become fused in a way that defies separation. After all, when you are in the middle of the crossroads it is impossible to say which road you are on. Achebe uses the fact that he is "perfectly bilingual" (34), as a result of his own dual linguistic heritage (Igbo and English), to illustrate this hybrid condition. According to Achebe, because of the power found at the crossroads, it is a place of danger and promise; "a man might perish there," but he also "might be lucky and return to his people with the boon of prophetic vision" (*Hopes* 34). If, as Obi Okonkwo's story suggests, cultural hybridity can result in disaster, in this particular legacy of colonialism resides one of the greatest promises for a better, decolonized future.

Both Achebe's reference to the man who *returns* to "his people" and the equation of his own bilingualism with the crossroads, emphasizes that for those who have been most fully hybridized as a result of education, the danger and the promise of the crossroads is most applicable. For Achebe, those with colonial educations can lead their people into a better future "with the boon of prophetic vision," even if their hybridity also constantly

threatens their survival. The potential elitism of this position is undermined by the representation of Obi in *No Longer At Ease*. Precisely what
leads him to "perish" and prevents him from being able to "return to his
people with the boon of prophetic vision" is his belief in his superiority
resulting from his upbringing and education. However, it cannot be
ignored that in privileging the educated hybrid Achebe threatens to vali-
date the very kind of hierarchical mindset which his novel castigates. To
some degree, this threat is imbedded in the form of the novel itself. Written in English and utilizing many of the conventions of the modernist
novel, it is obviously geared towards an audience of highly educated Nigerians. Commenting on the readership of this novel, Achebe said that
while he did not "have a foreign audience in mind. [. . .] Most of [his]
readers are young. They are either in school or college or have only
recently left. And many of them look to [him] as a kind of teacher" (*Hopes*
41). Although Achebe claims to write to a Nigerian audience, this audience only includes the small portion of Nigerians who would have had
enough "school or college" to enable them to read *No Longer At Ease*. The
fact that *No Longer At Ease* is addressed to an educated elite means it has
the potential—especially in conjunction with the large body of similarly
focused Europhone African literature of the 1960s—to reinforce a sense
of their own centrality and class identification. In other words, as part of
a whole body of Europhone-African literature, *No Longer At Ease* contributes (albeit indirectly) to the division between the elites and the rest
of the national community. One result of this division is, of course, an
exacerbation of neocolonialism. In this sense, Achebe's novel fundamentally contradicts itself because what it criticizes and warns against on one
level, it reinforces on another. As a result of its language and form, the
novel militates against the kind of interdependent, egalitarian national
community it cries out for at the level of content. This contradiction suggests what a difficult task it is to construct a new national community that
moves beyond the patterns laid out by colonial policy and ideology.

2

Under Kenyan Eyes

Ngugi wa Thiong'o's Re-Vision
of *Under Western Eyes*

Kwame Appiah has denounced as nativist the notion that "African literature *is* an autonomous entity separate and apart from all other literature" (56–57).[1] Appiah claims this idea of a pure literary tradition, based on a "topology of inside and outside—indigene and alien, western and traditional," ignores that literary traditions are never pure because they are always impacted by outside influences. He further suggests this misconception stems from a European ideology of nationalism in which the nation and its culture is viewed as springing from a shared racial or ethnic essence. Frederick Buell takes up a similar argument in *National Culture and the New Global System.* He questions "the discourse of cultural imperialism" which portrays non-Western traditional cultures as endangered, threatened from the outside (7–8). Buell argues that the notion of autonomous primordial cultures embedded in this discourse ends up duplicating colonialist thought by portraying those cultures as weak and premodern. He suggests what is masked by such a notion is that "local cultures do not simply exist prior to and apart from global forces, but owe their contemporary existence to them" (34). In other words, to suggest there are rigidly bound traditional cultures in danger of contamination by exterior forces both misrepresents the ways cultures actually develop and reinforces a conceptual model which is an important part of imperialist ideology.

Of course, literary relationships between African and European texts inevitably invoke precisely such questions of cultural purity and decolonization. One such relationship, between Ngugi wa Thiong'o's *A Grain of Wheat* and the work of Joseph Conrad, has generated a particularly large body of criticism devoted to exploring the significance of this relationship for *A Grain of Wheat*'s cultural status.[2] Commenting on his early attraction to Conrad's fiction, Ngugi himself has said Conrad inspired him because, although English was not Conrad's native tongue, his place in the British canon was firmly established: "Was he not already an image of what we, the new African writers, like the Irish writers before us, Yeats and the others, could become?" (*Moving* 5).[3] Yet despite this affinity, Ngugi found himself at odds with Conrad as a result of their contrasting positions with respect to colonialism: "Conrad had chosen to be part of the empire and the moral ambivalence in his attitude towards British imperialism stems from that chosen allegiance" (6). In this respect, Ngugi claims greater identification with writers such as George Lamming who speak from the position of having been under British colonial domination: "Lamming, unlike Conrad, wrote very clearly from the other side of the empire, from the side of those who were crying 'Let My People Go.' Conrad always made me uneasy with his inability to see any possibility of redemption arising from the energy of the oppressed" (6). If Ngugi admired Conrad and felt some connection with him, he also recognized the dangers of Conrad's perspective for those fighting colonialism.

One possible reading of the links between *A Grain of Wheat* and *Heart of Darkness* is that they constitute a retort in which Ngugi uses Conrad to evoke a European colonial vision to which he writes back. In particular, Ngugi uses the Kurtz-like District Officer Thompson in order to ridicule British colonial ideology. Like Kurtz, Thompson goes to Africa with a triumphalist notion of the British Empire and a corresponding sense of his own heroic "destiny dressed in the form of an idea" (53). This "idea" is the project of disseminating British culture and transforming Europe's others into British subjects. He records his reflections on the British empire in notes he intends to publish as a book, *Prospero in Africa*. His initial scribblings, like the majority of Kurtz's report to the International Society for the Suppression of Savage Customs, offer the image of a benevolent, godlike colonial master smoothly improving the condition of benighted (and grateful) Africans: "To administer to a people is to administer to a soul" (55). In Africa, however, he becomes increasingly savage in response to what he sees as the "anarchy" and "savagery" of the Mau Mau rebellion, declaring in his notes, "One must use a stick" (55). Eventually, he becomes a vicious commandant of a prisoncamp where the result of all his fine sentiments are summed up by his proclamation to "Eliminate the vermin" (134)—a strong echo of Kurtz's call to "Exterminate the Brutes."

Andrea White reads these echoes of *Heart of Darkness* as evidence that Ngugi is drawing on Conrad to further his effort to counter colonial discourse: "That Conrad's work contributed significantly to the 'writing back' of decolonization is attested to be such writers as Ngugi himself whose writing has been compared to that of Conrad" (201). White suggests that by creating an administator modeled on Kurtz, Ngugi draws on Conrad's condemnation of the type of colonial man Kurtz represents. This reading makes sense, but only up to a point. In *A Grain of Wheat,* the problem for Thompson is that his absolutely monologic colonial vision cannot account for either the existence of a viable non-European culture or for the desire among the colonized to create their own nations free from British control. As a result, Kenyans appear to him as perverse and incomprehensible; they can only be a force of "anarchy" and "evil" which must be violently crushed. In contrast with *A Grain of Wheat, Heart of Darkness* does not represent Africans as people with a civilization of their own who could or would want to rule themselves. (Consider, for example, their despair over the thought of Kurtz, their god and leader, leaving.) In fact, they are represented as part of the anarchy and savagery of the African wilderness which beckons to Kurtz's own buried, brutal desires. In this sense, *Heart of Darkness* reinscribes some of the same principles of colonial discourse which Ngugi ridicules, and the echoes of Conrad's novella in *A Grain of Wheat* can be read as enabling a condemnation of those principles through the process of writing back to *Heart of Darkness.*

However, if the notion that Ngugi uses Conrad to write back to the colonizer works with the echoes of *Heart of Darkness,* it is not satisfying in terms of the relationship between *A Grain of Wheat* and *Under Western Eyes,* since the latter Conradian text does not really deal with colonialism and, especially, not with colonialism in Africa. Critics offer an extensive catalogue of many similarities between the novels, especially in terms of plot, characterization, and theme. Often, they insist the differences are more pronounced and more important than the similarities—in order to assert the value of *A Grain of Wheat* as an original piece of literature. For example, Ponnuthurai Sarvan insists Ngugi's novel "does have the right to be considered an original work" (156) and Bu-Buakei Jabbi argues that Ngugi's "own creative individuality, far from being flushed out by the influences it may accommodate, continually asserts itself with frequent originality of effect; and sometimes it even transcends some source of inspiration that may be clearly discerned" (80).[4] This line of argument seems to somehow extricate the influence of Conrad's novel and judge what is left—what belongs "purely" to Ngugi.

On the other hand, certain critics assert the use of Conrad compromises some of Ngugi's own goals because the ideology embedded in *Under Western Eyes* infects Ngugi's novel. Ebele Obumselu argues "*A Grain of Wheat* is a radically divided work" because "Ngugi identified with Kihika [a symbol of revolutionary values in the novel] but he still retained the plot which Conrad devised to show the futility and ironic contradictions of revolutionary nationalism" (114–115). David Maughan-Brown asserts that Ngugi's attempt to affirm the value of community over that of the individual "is betrayed by the [. . .] choice of the plot of *Under Western Eyes*" (251). According to these critics, Ngugi's reliance on Conrad's novel frustrates his desire to assert the value of a collective revolutionary movement because *Under Western Eyes* valorizes individual consciousness above collective consciousness and suggests that all revolutions will end in failure. The underlying assumption is that the cultural purity of Ngugi's Kenyan novel has been violated by the intrusive European elements of Conrad's text. Those elements are *not* extricable, and Ngugi's novel is the worse for it.

What is missing from this body of criticism is consideration of the notion that using *Under Western Eyes* as a model might have itself been part of the inventiveness and originality of Ngugi's creative process. Far from allowing his novel to become colonized when he chose Conrad's text as a model, Ngugi appropriated Conrad for an African cultural tradition—undermining, in the process, the notion of essential national character embedded in *Under Western Eyes.* Furthermore, debates over how to evaluate Ngugi's use of Conrad leave little room for discussion of the significance in Ngugi's novel of neocolonialism or of the fears of the long-term effects of colonial and capitalist ideology on the formation of Kenyan consciousness.[5] In part, this may be the result of the critics' desire to stress the enormous gulf between the two writers' political and philosophical visions and their relative geographical and historical positions. For example, Bu-Buakei Jabbi claims "Conradian influence is minimal on the political" theme in *A Grain of Wheat* because that theme derives "from the general historical experience of late colonial Kenya in which Ngugi grew up" (53).[6] Felix Mnthali cautions that the danger in tracing the links between Conrad's and Ngugi's work "is that of creating an almost watertight neatness which ignores the gulf between Conrad's skepticism and Ngugi's commitment to change" (91).[7] Although they ignore the significance of neocolonialism for the connection between *Under Western Eyes* and *A Grain of Wheat,* these critics make an important point: Ngugi and Conrad are separated by vast differences in political and historical perspective. However, part of the strength of Ngugi's novel lies precisely in the way he utilizes Conrad's plot, characterization, and themes to warn against both neocolonialism and the long-term dangers of colonial and capitalist ideology, while transforming the political significance of Conrad's story by altering its representations of essential national and racial identity, collective and individual progress, and revolution. In other words, part of the originality of Ngugi's novel lies in his critical appropriation of Conrad's text into an evolving Kenyan culture.

In terms of plot and characterization, the similarities between *A Grain of Wheat* and *Under Western Eyes* have been so clearly (and exhaustively) established in the critical corpus discussed above they need only be sketched here.[8] Both Razumov and Mugo lack families, focus on private aspirations, and invite confidences as a result of their reticence. Both betray revolutionary heroes who confide in them, and then, ironically, are themselves mistaken as revolutionary heroes. Both establish friendships with the trusting, beautiful sisters of the betrayed revolutionary heroes, and as a result of their relationships with these sisters both finally make public confessions of their guilt. As Sarvan puts it, "Ngugi's story, like that of Conrad's, is set amidst a political struggle waged against oppression and is concerned with betrayal and confession" (154).

The significance of this intertextual connection is found in the imperative of Ngugi's warning against neocolonialism. In *A Grain of Wheat,* Ngugi wants to make his readers see the dangers of betrayal and disillusionment within a newly liberated Kenya, and the plot and characterization of *Under Western Eyes* work wonderfully to get such a message across. Conrad's text depicts an authoritarian political structure that shapes the perceptions of those under its control, even those who most openly oppose it. And the novel explores the potential for betrayal that results from the difficulty of escaping that structure's influence and from callous self-interest. Similarly, Ngugi's novel represents the possibility of the betrayal of the ideals and goals of the national liberation movement by those who came to power in newly independent Kenya, precisely because they are still controlled by self-interest and conceptions of social and political relations determined by a repressive political structure—in this case colonialism.

Yet, if Ngugi found *Under Western Eyes* useful as a textual model, the worldview implicit in Conrad's novel is nevertheless antithetical to the goal of asserting the need for continued resistance to colonialism and colonial ideology in a newly independent Kenya. The origins of Conrad's worldview are found not only—and perhaps not even primarily—in his personal philosophical skepticism concerning change, but also in deeply entrenched nationalist and imperialist conceptions of the world as they were linked with Britain's geopolitical position in Conrad's time, Britain's relationship with Russia, and Conrad's attitudes towards both countries. At the turn of the century, Britain and Russia were imperial powers which utilized what Hugh Seton-Watson calls "official nationalism" to legitimate and control their empires (148). Official nationalism legitimized a ruling dynasty and an empire by linking them with notions of nation and national character; subject peoples were to be made part of the nation culturally and linguistically through educational and cultural policy. As Benedict Anderson asserts, "These 'official nationalisms' can best be understood as a means for [. . .] stretching the short, tight skin of the nation over the gigantic body of the empire" (86). Thus, in the later half of the nineteenth century there is the Russification and Anglicization of Russia's and England's respective empires. Despite this similarity, however, a strong antipathy towards Russia prevailed in Britain at the turn of the century. In Britain, the Russophobia prominent throughout much of the nineteenth century was exacerbated by the perception of Russia as a potential rival for imperial power in Asia (Hyam 261–265). Conrad loathed the Russians because of his family's suffering under Russia's imperial rule and his feelings concerning Polish nationalism; the Russophobia in Britain would have only further stoked his hatred.

Given these factors, it is not surprising Under Western Eyes creates a clear, unbridgeable distance between Britain and Russia politically, socially, and culturally. The novel obscures similarities between the two countries' imperial structures and policies by representing this distance as the result of inalterably different sensibilities, perspectives, and conceptions of the world as determined by national character. In other words, the representation of the relationship between Russia and the rest of Europe in Under Western Eyes facilitates condemnation of Russia's political, social, and cultural identity while masking the connections Russia's power structures had to the power structures of the rest of Europe. Furthermore, the idea that the Russian national character necessarily led to a despotic and corrupt autocracy both allows an attack on that authoritarian structure and an undermining of the social revolutionary impulse. Given the link between national character and political rule, real change could only come about through the evolution of the national character itself (rather than through revolution). In other words, the representation of an impermeable boundary between Western Europe and Russia is an excellent way to delegitimize Russia's right to empire without questioning the legitimacy of other European empires or advocating revolution.

Finally, the degree to which Conrad's text is read as an endorsement of any model of development, it remains tied to imperial conceptions of progress because of its representation of national character. Numerous critics point out that colonial ideology includes rigid definitions of ethnic and racial identities because these definitions are the means of differentiating peoples on a developmental timeline. As Edward Said argues:

> Neither imperialism nor colonialism is a simple act of accumulation and acquisition. Both are supported [. . .] by impressive ideological formations that include notions that certain territories and people *require* and beseech domination, as well as forms of knowledge affiliated with domination. (9)

Such "territories and people" can only progress when they become like the West—when they allow themselves to be tutored as the Russian girl Natalia in *Under Western Eyes* is tutored by the British narrator. In *Under Western Eyes*, Britain is able to bring progress to its colonies and the world in general because of its relative level of development, while Russia is a threat to the world and brings devolution not evolution.

In *Under Western Eyes*, the absolute distance between Russian autocracy and Western European political and social models is represented by the narrator as resulting from clearly definable national characteristics that place Russia well behind the rest of Europe in a teleology of development. The narrator postulates that Western readers will have a difficult time understanding his story because they are so far removed from the cruelty and irrationality of a regressive political and social structure:

> For this is a Russian story for Western ears, which, as I have observed already, are not attuned to certain tones of cynicism and cruelty, or moral negation, and even of moral distress already silenced at our end of Europe. (180)

According to the narrator, the temporal distance between Russia and the West and the resulting epistemological gap cannot simply be ascribed to a difference in institutions; the Russian intellect itself has failed to develop. He claims to have "no comprehension of the Russian character" because of "the illogicality of [Russians'] attitude, the arbitrariness of their conclusion"(56). The result is Russians have produced a horrific form of government, which perpetuates their moral and intellectual stagnation. When discussing the thoughts and fears that lead to Razumov's betrayal of the revolutionary Haldin, the narrator proclaims,

> Nations it may be have fashioned their Governments, but the Governments have paid them back in the same coin. It is unthinkable that any young Englishman should find himself in Razumov's situation. This being so it would be a vain enterprise to imagine what he would think. The only safe surmise is that he would not think as Mr. Razumov thought at this crisis of his fate. He would not have an hereditary and personal knowledge of the means by which a historical autocracy represses ideas, guards its power, and defends its existence. (72)

Although the narrator emphasizes that the difference between British and Russian subjectivities is the result of different political systems, he still suggests this difference is a product of alien national characters by foregrounding the assertion that "nations [. . .] have fashioned their Governments."

The hopelessness the narrator finds in the Russian political situation is exacerbated by his belief that revolution, rather than enabling progress, is always a destructive, regressive force. Indeed, he often links revolution with the horrible autocratic Russian government, claiming both are "lawless" (113). He asserts revolution unshackles personal ambition and greed and leads to the betrayal of hopes and ideals: "in a real revolution—not a simple dynastic change or a mere reform of institutions—in a real revolution the best characters do not come to the front. [. . .] Hopes grotesquely betrayed, ideals caricatured—that is the definition of revolutionary success" (153).[9]

In such a world, individual growth among Russians can be measured solely in terms of an effort to acknowledge and remain loyal to the truth of their own lives; thus, growth for Razumov lies in his confession of his betrayal of Haldin because he reveals an unwillingness to live a life of falsehood. As Sophia Antonovna points out,

> It was just when he believed himself safe and more—infinitely more—when the possibility of being loved by that admirable girl first dawned upon him, that he discovered that his bitterest rail-

ings, the worst wickedness, the devil work of hate and pride, could never cover up the ignominy of the existence before him. There's character in such discovery. (347–348)

However, a crucial aspect of Razumov's growth includes an acknowledgment of the absolute and inevitable degeneracy in Russian civil and political society. As he says to Natalia, "I have managed to remain amongst the truth of things and the realities of life—our Russian life—such as they are" (321). The "truth of things" in *Under Western Eyes* is autocracy and revolution are equally and necessarily corrupt, and Russia remains mired in a primitive political and moral morass. As a result, individual growth cannot lead to a viable and legitimate Russian social or political model. The knowledge Razumov gives to Natalia gives the narrator no hope for the future, even though it allows Natalia to grow personally. Looking into her eyes, the narrator observes,

> Shadows seemed to come and go in them as if the steady flame of her soul had been made to vacillate at last in the cross-currents of poisoned air from the corrupted dark immensity claiming her for its own, where virtues themselves fester into crime in the cynicism of oppression and revolt. (329)

In contrast with Conrad's novel, *A Grain of Wheat* challenges the notion of a primordial national essence or character. In the new postindependence Kenyan nation, the belief that the age of colonialism is over simply because the British have left becomes a threat to the interests of a majority of Kenyans, since it will mask the need for resistance against neocolonialism. As a result, *A Grain of Wheat* strives to unlink a particular national or racial identity (British) from a particular repressive form of governance (colonialism). (This divorcing of essential collective character and political structure contrasts sharply with the notion in *Under Western Eyes* that there is a necessary and causal relationship between autocracy and the Russian character.) While *A Grain of Wheat* is certainly concerned with the effects of underdevelopment under colonialism, the danger at the moment of decolonization is that, despite the departure of the British, colonial and capitalist structures and ideology will continue to shape Kenyans' perceptions.[10] Colonialism will continue under black colonial masters working with white settlers and European powers; Kenyans will now construct the policies which underdevelop Kenya.[11] The theme of the betrayal of a revolution, stemming from deep-rooted ideological structures and from self-interest, is precisely what makes

Conrad's text so useful to Ngugi. Furthermore, by explicitly using *Under Western Eyes* as a model for a novel concerned with the forging of a Kenyan national community, Ngugi undermines the notion of a primordial national character—embodied in a pure traditional culture—that is one of the assumptions of *Under Western Eyes*.

Throughout *A Grain of Wheat*, colonial and capitalist structures and ideology lead directly to betrayal because they suggest the only important bonds between people are based on a colonizer/colonized model or on the business contract. Suppressing the possibility of other kinds of bonds, colonialism and capitalism encourage atomization and result in the lack of a sense of common goals and responsibilities among all Kenyans. We clearly see the lingering danger of colonial ideology in the betrayal of Kihika by Mugo, a parallel of the betrayal of Haldin by Razumov in *Under Western Eyes*. After Kihika comes to Mugo to hide from the police, Mugo decides to turn Kihika in; through his musings it is clear Mugo conceives of power in colonial terms—that is, as separated from any identification with or sense of responsibility to the Kenyan community. Mugo thinks to himself

> What's power? A judge is powerful: he can send a man to death, without anyone questioning his authority, judgment, or harming his body in return. Yes—to be great you must stand in such a place that you can dispense pain and death to others without anyone asking questions. Like a headmaster, a judge, a Governor. (197)

Mugo conceives of these public figures only in terms of the ability to wield authority without accountability ("without anyone asking questions"). The absence of accountability is, for Mugo, the mark of "great"-ness.

Gikonyo, meanwhile, represents the Kenyan entrepreneur who embraces capitalist ideology:

> But if he promptly fulfilled his part of the contract, he expected no less from the other side. Thus he insisted on getting the money at the agreed day and time. He would not countenance a delay. He treated the rich and poor alike. [. . .] But they trusted and came to respect his scrupulous honesty. At least he did fulfill, on time, his own part of the bargain. (57)

The narrow notion of responsibility dictated by the business contract encourages Gikonyo to exploit his own people. He buys and hoards bags of staples during the harvest, and then when such staples are scarce he sells them. Gikonyo is a significant threat to Kenya not only because he becomes wealthy by manipulating his people's needs and perpetuating the effects of colonial policy, but also because he becomes the means of glorifying the capitalist worldview: "The story of Gikonyo's rise to wealth, although on a small scale, carried a moral every mother in Thabai pointed out to her children" (59).

Since the traditional colonial model is no longer in place after the departure of the British, the capitalist perspective Gikonyo represents is, perhaps, the most significant ideological danger for Kenya. If Kenya accepts him as its hero, as a representative of its values, then the result is a society structured around self-interest, which enables those with power and wealth to identify Kenya's progress with their own. As a minority group continues to advance materially and politically at the expense of the rest of the nation, they actually become part of the "First World" which benefits from the underdevelopment of the "Third World" (thus rendering those terms useless as designations for geographical regions). The result is the betrayal of the majority of the Kenyan people. This threat is made explicit in the character of the district M.P. who cuts himself off from those he represents. He does not come to the Uhuru celebrations in the villages, but remains in the capital to entertain foreign dignitaries: "You see, we have so many foreign guests to look after. So apologize to the people for me and say I can't come," the M.P. tells Gikonyo (63). Such a development is not surprising, however, given the M.P.s' isolation from their own constituencies: "Few M.P.s had offices in their constituencies. As soon as they were elected, they ran to Nairobi and were rarely seen in their areas, except when they came back with other national leaders to address big political rallies" (60). The result of such a structure is a lack of any sense of communal responsibility by those in power.

Rather than positing a pre-existing Kenyan character as the basis for a new society, *A Grain of Wheat* suggests that a truly *postcolonial* Kenyan nation necessitates forging a collective culture and consciousness through a common, evolving history, as defined by the interrelated histories of its members.[12] As a result, the sharing of personal histories and secrets, often through storytelling, is a critical condition for personal and communal progress. After Mumbi and Gikonyo have told Mugo their stories of the misery of the villagers during the emergency, the horrors of the prison camp, the effects of the death of Kihika (which Mugo helped bring about), and their own stories of misery and betrayal, Mugo cannot deny his connection with the village and his responsibility for his actions:

he was irrevocably drawn to the lives of the villagers. He tried to think of something else [. . .] but he could not escape from his knowledge of Gikonyo's and Mumbi's lives. [. . .] How was it that Mumbi's story had cracked open his dulled inside and released imprisoned thoughts and feelings? (172)

Mumbi's and Gikonyo's stories have made it impossible for Mugo to separate the trajectory of his life from the trajectories of "the lives of the villagers" which (understood as necessarily intertwined) define a communal history.

The feelings of connection Mumbi inspires eventually lead Mugo to confess his betrayal of Kihika to her: "She had sat there, and talked to him and given him a glimpse of a new earth. She had trusted him, and confided in him. This simple trust had forced him to tell her the truth" (234). Mugo's glimpse of a "new earth," a community which entails common history, responsibilities, and goals, brings about his public confession to the entire community. Mugo finds a new "vision" of his "purpose" in life: to share his secret, and so his true history, with the community (235). This discovery occurs not because Mugo recognizes an ahistorical or transhistorical national character which subsumes him—Razumov's realization in *Under Western Eyes*—but because he acknowledges his historically determined interrelatedness with the community and accepts and even desires the implications of that interrelatedness.

His confession is also an act of self-sacrifice for the good of that community; Mugo is compelled to admit his crime to the villagers, rather than just to Mumbi, when they sing at his hut on the night of Uhuru, believing him to be a hero who embodies the virtues of the liberation movement:

And then suddenly he heard the village people around his hut singing Uhuru songs. Every word of praise carried for him a piercing irony. What had he done for the village? What had he done for anybody? (235)

Throughout the text, this kind of irony is a sign of a threat to the community because it results from trusting individuals and values most dangerous to the community as a whole. By confessing to the community, Mugo collapses one example of this kind of irony and strengthens the community by helping to cleanse the culture of a false hero.

Ultimately, however, the basis for hope in *A Grain of Wheat* lies not in Mugo's act of self-sacrifice, but in his transformation in the memories and stories of his people into a new kind of hero embodying new values.[13] As

Peter Nazareth points out, an important difference between Razumov's and Mugo's deaths is the effect that they have on their communities: "Razumov's confession does not have a positive impact on anybody while Mugo's confession shows others the way. For if he was so courageous as to lay open his terrible secret before all, can others not bare their souls to one another?" (251). Kenya already has heroes like Kihika who embody values such as a willingness for sacrifice in the pursuit of common goals. But the new nation now needs heroic figures who represent the notion of sacrifice through public confession because of the growing irony of false heroes. At the moment of Uhuru, the danger represented by this irony is persistent: the very men most likely to betray the Kenyan community as a whole, those focused on gaining personal power and wealth, are those who will prosper and thus be praised. Progress in Kenya, therefore, requires a focus not only on the recognition of the individual's inextricable links with the larger Kenyan community (along with the responsibilities such links entail) but also on a concomitant willingness to openly integrate the personal self with the communal self through the sharing of personal stories and secrets. As in *Under Western Eyes,* individual growth in *A Grain of Wheat* involves a willingness to recognize and express the truth of one's history, but, in contrast with Conrad's novel, here such growth cannot be separated from the promise of a new and better sociopolitical model.[14]

If Mugo's confession symbolically embodies values which help combat neocolonialism, then the policy of retributive bloodletting as a means of cleansing the new nation is represented by Ngugi as both useless and dangerous. General R., Lt. Koina, Warui, and Wambui hold a secret military tribunal which finds Mugo guilty of treason and results in his execution. In the last scene with Wambui, images of invading darkness and filth foreshadow the danger to Kenya if this form of sacrifice, rather than Mugo's, becomes the norm:

> Darkness was creeping into the hut. Wambui was lost in a solid consciousness of a terrible anti-climax to her activities in the fight for freedom. Perhaps we should not have tried him [Mugo], she muttered. Then she shook herself, trying to bring her thoughts to the present. I must light the fire. First I must sweep the room. How dirt can so quickly collect in a clean hut! But she did not rise to do anything. (243)

This scene suggests that a focus on vengence, especially against individuals, prevents the new nation from being able to sweep itself clean of the destructive legacies of colonialism. As Kihika says, "In Kenya we want deaths which will change things, that is to say, we want true sacrifice" (95). Efforts to create a sacrificial scapegoat (whose execution supposedly rids the community of the threat of betrayal) works against the crucial principle of collective responsibility and facilitates neocolonialism by masking the deeply embedded ideological and structural forces on which it feeds. In his condemnation of the use of scapegoats, Ngugi creates another important parallel with *Under Western Eyes.* When Razumov confesses his duplicity to the revolutionaries, he is also violently punished by having his eardrums ruptured by the menacing revolutionary enforcer Nikita. The horrible irony of this act of retribution is that, while Razumov renders himself harmless to the revolutionaries by his act of confession, Nikita turns out to be a double agent. Even more important, the focus on punishing an individal, self-confessed "traitor" suggests a complete lack of recognition of the deeper forces of betrayal at play among the Russian revolutionaries. If Ngugi and Conrad have very different visions of the potential benefits of violent revolution, then they share a similar perspective on the dangers of retributive justice for any hope of a liberated nation.

In *A Grain of Wheat,* this hope is most fully suggested in the last section of the novel entitled "Harambee" or coming together—a reference to the slogan of Kenya's government at the moment of liberation. As he sits in his hospital bed, Gikonyo thinks about what Mugo has done and applies it to his own sense of guilt for betraying the liberation movement:

> For the last three days he thought of Mugo and the confession. Could he, Gikonyo, gather such courage to tell people about the steps on the pavement? [. . .] Mugo had the courage to face his guilt and lose everything. Gikonyo shuttered at the thought of losing everything. (245)

As a result of his reflections on Mugo's confession, Gikonyo begins the healing process with his estranged wife Mumbi by being willing to listen and open his heart to her: "After Mugo's confession, he found himself trying to puzzle out Mumbi's thoughts and feelings. . . . He increasingly longed to speak to her about Mugo and then about his own life in detention" (245). In this extremely symbolic text, the promise of reconciliation through sharing stories represents the hope that Kenya will be able to combat the neocolonialism foreshadowed in the text, in part by forging a collective culture that counters the values of self-interest and exploitation. The centrality of culture is emphasized in the last chapter by references to Gikonyo's design for a stool. While in detention, he decides he wants to carve a stool for Mumbi with its three legs representing three men toiling separately: "The seat would rest on three legs curved into three grim-faced figures, sweating under a weight" (244). This design represents men working alone, without connection or common goal. However, after the beginning of his reconciliation with Mumbi, Gikonyo conceives of the three legs as representing members of a family—father, mother, and child—all touching one another, all connected, with the woman's figure being pregnant. The carving signifies hope for Kenya through an image of a family working together for the future.

As discussions of Mugo's role as a hero and the development of Gikonyo's stool suggest, if hope in *A Grain of Wheat* is rooted in a (revolutionary) sense of communal consciousness that enables members of the community to break free from the prison of isolating individualism and self-interest, such hope is inextricably bound to a constantly evolving culture which develops from that communal consciousness. This conception of how culture and collective identity are produced is profoundly anti-nativist: it suggests that neither is fixed and that both evolve in a reciprocal relationship. Frantz Fanon claims that what makes a culture authentic is not its adherence to unadulterated tradition, but its relationship to a people's efforts to forge themselves into a collectivity:

> A national culture is not a folklore, nor an abstract populism that believes it can discover the people's true nature. [. . .] A national culture is the whole body of efforts made by a people in the sphere of thought to describe, justify, and praise the action through which that people has created itself and keeps itself in existence. (233)

Significantly, Ngugi was strongly influenced by Fanon in the writing of *A Grain of Wheat;*[15] thus it is not surprising that, as Frederick Buell convincingly argues, *A Grain of Wheat* itself attacks the notion that an originary, essential African culture which could be returned to even exists (87–100). Instead, Ngugi's novel represents the forging of a Kenyan culture, and part of this culture includes the integration—and transformation—of elements of European culture. In other words, an "authentic" African revolutionary culture is not defined by its purity from European influences. For example, in the novel, Kihika reinterprets Christianity in

order to encourage Kenyans to unite and to fight, and if necessary to die,
so that all Kenyans can be free. He insists Christ should be understood in
Kenya not as an individual, but as a collective:

> Everybody who takes the Oath of Unity to change things in
> Kenya is a Christ. Christ then is not one person. All those who
> take up the cross of liberating Kenya are the true Christs for us
> Kenyan people. (95)

While drawing on and reconfiguring the symbolism of Christ as a figure
who suffers and struggles for others, Kihika magnifies the collectivity suggested in that symbolism. In doing so, he takes a European religion and
transforms it into an inspiration for the struggle for a free Kenya.

The reciprocal relationship between an ever-evolving Kenyan culture,
which appropriates and transforms useful elements of Western European
culture, and the development of a new Kenya is emblematized in the narration of Ngugi's text, which incorporates elements of the oral tradition
into the form of the novel. At the same time, this narration suggests
another way *A Grain of Wheat* appropriates and transforms *Under Western Eyes;* both novels include a narrator who is a character reporting a
story to a specific audience with which that narrator identifies. One
aspect of Conrad's work which must have appealed to Ngugi was his ability to utilize such a narrator in a convincing fashion. However, as with the
other elements of *Under Western Eyes,* there were aspects of Conrad's narration which were antithetical to the primary narrative goals of *A Grain
of Wheat.*

The British schoolteacher of Conrad's novel tells a story of Eastern
Europe to a Western European audience, and he supports that audience's
notion of itself, as we have seen, by creating an unbridgeable gap between
Western Europe and the horrors of Russian autocracy. This perspective is
achieved because the narrator gives order and meaning to Razumov's story
(partly accessed through the latter's diary) by contextualizing it in terms
of a concept of the world that represents Western Europe as a locus of
progress and order. The narrator also reinforces a division of intellectual
work. He is an intellectual (a schoolteacher with extensive knowledge of
Western European literature) who places himself in a position of authority in respect to his audience as a result of a special knowledge that he pos-
sesses but they do not.

In contrast, as Thomas Jackson notes,

> The narrator of *A Grain of Wheat* takes no part whatsoever in the
> action, but he speaks often in the first person plural, as if address-
> ing or speaking of a familiar community. (9)

The narrator of Ngugi's novel is a member of a Gikuyu village who
speaks as an equal to other members of that village and tells a story of
their common history. He or she is not part of an intellectual class laying claim to the attention of the audience because of a superiority of
knowledge and experience; instead, this storyteller constantly reminds
his or her audience that they all share knowledge of the story that is
being told. The notion of a division of intellectual and artistic labor is
undermined, since the audience becomes part of the story and the telling
of the story.[16]

The voice of the narrator increasingly gains strength in the course of
the novel. Throughout much of the first half of the text there is a standard third person omniscient narration, albeit one rooted in a Gikuyu
consciousness. This consciousness is made more explicit as the narrator
increases his or her direct comments to the Gikuyu audience, as if he or
she were seated before that audience and were inviting participation in the
telling of the story. Especially in the second half of the novel, he or she
intersperses the narrative with phrases such as "You remember," "our people," "our hard-won freedom," "this our land," and "most of us from
Thabai" (178), as well as references to shared memories, history, geogra-
phy, and communal identity. Significantly, the oral storytelling form
becomes more explicit at roughly the same pace that Mugo is represented
as becoming aware of his connections with the community and the link
between his history and theirs; as Mugo gains a more communally based
consciousness, so does the form of the novel. This parallel development
suggests revolutionary culture is not static, but is forever evolving; new
cultural forms arise as the existing culture is fused with new forms of communal consciousness.

Part of this evolution in *A Grain of Wheat* involves fusion of the oral
tradition with the novel form. As Ngugi's novel suggests, that tradition
can have a reciprocally transformative relationship with a European cultural form. Through his use of orality, Ngugi links *A Grain of Wheat* with
a cultural practice of the majority of Kenyans, enacted to bind their communities, articulate their points of view, and tell their history. He also
resists that aspect of colonial ideology which denigrates non-Western cultural practices as less developed. At the same time, Ngugi strategically

appropriates a Western cultural form with which he had become familiar through his colonial and British education, in the service of building a new form of national collective consciousness—a goal facilitated by a published novel which would be more quickly and widely disseminated than a strictly oral story. The Western form is thus integrated into an evolving Kenyan culture. As Edward Sackey observes, Ngugi and other African writers

> depend on the oral tradition of Africa to deform the received Western novelistic pattern in order to challenge our received notion while our African identity is also affirmed, thereby freeing Africa from the negative image in which others have created us. (390)

Sackey suggests that growth for the African novelist can be defined in much the same way it is for the characters in *A Grain of Wheat:* a vigilance against blind acceptance of European practices and a movement towards an ever-developing communal and cultural consciousness (which in the case of the novelist includes utilization of, but not control by, some of those practices).

As argued throughout this chapter, Ngugi's critical use of *Under Western Eyes* in the writing of his own novel reflects this conception of African cultural development. He uses Conrad's text in the same way Kihika uses the bible: to help keep alive prospects for the evolution and progress of Kenya by incorporating aspects of the text that serve his ends and transforming those aspects that do not. Ngugi clearly found the plot and characterization of *Under Western Eyes* useful for demonstrating the permeation of colonial ideology into every aspect of Kenyan life and the consequent high risk of neocolonialism in a newly independent Kenya. However, the social and political vision of Conrad's novel could all too easily be read as discouraging the pursuit of revolutionary noncolonial social, cultural, and political structures or rejecting any kind of institutional communal structure whatsoever. By appropriating *Under Western Eyes,* an essentially individualistic and antirevolutionary novel, for collective and revolutionary purposes, Ngugi fundamentally revises Conrad's text.

A Grain of Wheat, then, suggests the cultures of the "Third World" have the strength to utilize and transform the culture of the "First World." Development and growth are not a return to an originary cultural identity any more than they are a complete capitulation to European and

American culture and identity. In *A Grain of Wheat*, progress involves struggling against forces which encourage and enable division among the people as a whole in Kenya; fighting exploitation by the First World both as a force in Kenya and outside of it; and developing forms and ideologies which help produce and empower a new community.

3

Legacies of Darkness

Neocolonialism and Conrad in Tayeb Salih's
Season of Migration to the North

The intertextual relationship between Joseph Conrad's fiction and Tayeb Salih's *Season of Migration to the North* has been read as one more case in point of the effort by the formerly colonized to write back to Conrad and the empire using a combative form of intertextuality. Saree Makdisi asserts:

> Just as Conrad's novel was bound up with Britain's imperial project, Salih's participates (in an oppositional way) in the afterlife of the same project today, by "writing back" to the colonial power that once ruled the Sudan. (805)

Indeed, Makdisi claims Salih's novel "deliberately confronts *[Heart of Darkness]* from within" (815). Edward Said apparently agrees, arguing that one of Salih's primary goals is to reclaim Conrad's fictive territory and thereby articulate "some of the discrepancies and their imagined consequences muffled by Conrad's majestic prose" (212). For Said, this reclamation is part of a larger fight by postcolonial writers in general to achieve recognition "on the very same territory once ruled by a consciousness that assumed the subordination of a designated inferior" (210). However, because Said places Salih's novel in the context of such a struggle with the colonist, he, like Makdisi, fails to recognize that the real objects of scrutiny in *Season of Migration* are the Sudanese themselves, who have inculcated the colonial mindset and ignored their own particular manifestations of it (212).

Salih's novel retells the history of imperialism with an eye to the way this history is made to reveal the origins of late twentieth-century African neocolonialism and its mindset, inextricably linked with, but more covert than, the obvious destructive effects of early twentieth-century European and American colonial practice and ideology—the forms of colonialism Conrad represents.[1] In a pivotal passage from Salih's novel, the narrator reveals a key component of neocolonial ideology when he mistakenly conceives of colonialism as something easily eradicated by breaking free from the direct control of Europe:

> The fact that they came to our land, I know not why, does that mean that we should poison our present and our future? Sooner or later they will leave our country, just as many people throughout history left many countries. The railways, ships, hospitals, factories and schools will be ours and we'll speak their language without either a sense of guilt or a sense of gratitude. Once again we shall be as we were—ordinary people—and if we are lies we shall be lies of our own making. (49–50)

Because Said misrepresents the primary critical target of the novel, he misreads this passage as a mere assertion that territory must be reclaimed from the colonizer. In the context of the novel, however, the narrator's naive comments reflect precisely why neocolonialism is such a threat in *Season of Migration;* the Sudanese characters remain unaware of how deeply colonial ideology infiltrates everything colonialism brought with it. Thus, the narrator regards European languages and institutions as, in Anthony Appiah's words, "mere tools [. . .] that can be cleansed of the accompanying imperialist [. . .] modes of thought" (56).

To explore the full complexity of Salih's novel and his relationship with Conrad, we need to replace the oppositional model of intertextuality assumed by both Said and Makdisi. When Salih echoes Conrad, he is not doing so to write back to the West, either by using him as a foil to write against or by elaborating on Conrad's critique of turn-of-the-century imperialism and neocolonialism. Any convincing account of Conrad's influence on Salih's novel must ultimately take into careful consideration the particular historical moment the novel was produced. My argument is that Salih used certain Conradian elements to expose and attack the contradictions of late twentieth-century neocolonialism in Sudan, as well as to illustrate the effects of these contradictions.[2] However, Salih also reconfigures aspects of Conrad's fiction that might be antithetical to his own goals, such as Conrad's conceptions of women and non-Western peoples, of links between identity, race, and place, and of the possibility of collective enlightenment and progressive action. Through his recontextualizing and transformation of Conradian elements, Salih skirts the dangers Conrad might represent for a writer struggling towards the postcolonial.

At a lecture at the American University in Beirut in 1980, Salih asserted that a primary foreign influence on him "as far as form goes" in writing *Season of Migration to the North* was "Conrad in *Heart of Darkness* and *Nostromo*" (Amyuni 15). The result, as Peter Nazareth notes, is that "the Conradian echoes" in Salih's novel "are too deliberate on the part of the highly literate author to be missed" ("Narrator" 133–34). As the basic links between Conrad and *Season of Migration* have been established elsewhere, I will briefly outline them here. Like Conrad in so much of his fiction, Salih employs a narrator who tells an extremely disturbing story from his own experience to a group of auditors and uses that story to reflect on the significance of his experience. Furthermore, like many of Conrad's narrators, Salih's narrator includes the stories of others told in their own words, and the use of these other voices reinforces the breakdown in the notion of a stable truth embodied by a single perspective. The narrator's story has two main figures: himself and the Kurtz-like Mustafa Sa'eed. The connection between these two men is the Conradian secret doubling relationship in which the double figure, in this case Mustafa, feels compelled to tell his story to the narrator, and the narrator, in turn, tells the story of his double after the double's death or disappearance. Mustafa and the narrator have both received a British education and, as in many of Conrad's doubling relationships, the affinity they feel is partly determined by this common educational background.

In terms of links with specific works by Conrad, it is worth noting Salih echoes "The Secret Sharer" in the figure of his young, naive narrator whose equilibrium is upset by the doubling relationship and the story of a crime committed by the double. There are also connections between *Nostromo* and *Season of Migration;* for example, Mustafa, like Nostromo, is incredibly talented, universally admired, but secretly corrupt. In addition, both of these works are concerned with neocolonialism, although its form and, more importantly, the perspective from which it is represented are quite different.[3] As John Davidson points out, *Season of Migration*'s relationship with *Under Western Eyes* is also notable; in both novels, the hope of liberation is threatened by the mindset of a despotic social and political structure, especially as that mindset has been inculcated by an educational system.

Season of Migration is most clearly connected, however, to *Heart of Darkness*. Both works describe the impact of north-south journeys on the narrators and their doubles; these journeys take the characters into the heart of a territory understood by colonial ideology as representing some purely geographical and cultural other to the place from which the narrators and doubles come. As Mohammad Shaheen points out, "The journey of Mustafa Sa'eed [. . .] echoes Kurtz's journey, but in reverse. [. . .] Kurtz in the Congo is a colonizer and invader. [Mustafa] announces himself in England as conqueror and invader" (156). There are also striking similarities between Kurtz's Intended and Hosna (Mustafa's Sudanese, second wife), and between the relationships of the narrators to both the Kurtz/Mustafa figure and Hosna/the Intended. Finally, in *Season of Migration to the North*, there are strong echoes of both the river imagery and the patterns of light and dark from *Heart of Darkness*.

Establishing links between the two authors is only a first step, however, in explaining the relationship between them. As suggested earlier, Salih uses Conrad to explore the configurations of neocolonialism. Although Frantz Fanon's *The Wretched of the Earth* was published in 1961, before these configurations become fully apparent in much of the decolonized world, his chapter, "The Pitfalls of National Consciousness," so accurately described them, that Ngugi asserts African literature written in the sixties and seventies "cannot really be understood without a proper and thorough reading of" that chapter (66). As Fanon suggests, central to any definition of neocolonialism is the notion of the exploitation of the newly independent nation by native elites working with Western capitalism, who are primarily interested in their own power and financial gain rather than in the development of the nation as a whole: "To them, nationalization quite simply means the transfer into native hands of those unfair advantages which are a legacy of the colonial period" (Fanon 152). The role of the elites, as the business partners of the West, is ironically masked by their nationalist, anti-European rhetoric espousing the idea of the nation for the natives. This rhetoric becomes a means for the native bourgeoisie to replace Europeans in lucrative posts; and, at the same time, it suggests that the elites are working to rid the nation of control by Western interests:

We have said that the native bourgeoisie which comes to power uses its class aggressiveness to corner the positions formerly kept for foreigners. On the morrow of independence, in fact, it violently attacks colonial personalities. [. . .] It will fight to the bitter end against these people "who insult our dignity as a nation." (155)

The machinations of the native ruling class result in a split between the achievement of national liberation—the freeing of the previously colonized nation from direct political control—and true liberation from the ideology and exploitation of the structures of colonialism understood broadly: "History teaches us clearly that the battle against colonialism does not run straight away along the lines of nationalism" (Fanon 148).

We can discern the outlines of Fanon's sketch of neocolonialism in the particular postindependence history of Sudan, as described by Tim Niblock:

> The political history of the 1956–69 period [Sudan was given independence in 1956; *Season of Migration* was first published in 1969] was dominated by one central characteristic: political influence and authority rested with those social groupings which had benefited from the distribution of resources under the Condominium [Britain's particular form of governance/control over the Sudan]. As might be expected, therefore, those who framed government policy were not inclined to undertake a radical reformation of the country's socio-economic structure. The two kinds of imbalance or inequality which had become prominent under the Condominium—differentiating both regions of the country and social groupings within it—continued and, indeed, became more marked. [. . .] Those who ruled Sudan over these years sought to develop the country within the socio-economic structure which they had inherited from the Condominium era, with minor changes. (204)[4]

The exacerbation of inequality is, of course, in part the result of the native elites gaining control over government and business: "While the structure of the economy did not alter much, the period was marked by the greater indigenisation of business, ensuring the incorporation of the indigenous 'incipient bourgeoisie' into a position of partnership, rather than subordination" (Woodward 124). In Sudan, geographic imbalance was exacerbated not only by the increased concentration of wealth and power in Khartoum but also by the north-south split in the country (which is not touched on directly in Salih's novel) (Woodward 126). Such increased urbanization and centralization at the expense of the rest of the country is another aspect of neocolonialism.

Season of Migration is particularly concerned with the way neocolonialism in Sudan thrives on what Ngugi calls a "reductionism to the polarities of colour and race" which result in colonialism being identified with the "whiteman" and anticolonial struggle with resistance to "European ways of perceiving and reacting to reality" (63). Salih emphasizes the links between such reductionism and both European colonial ideology and Sudanese traditionalism, which are connected by an epistemology that organizes the world in terms of rigid and natural definitions and boundaries, especially as they are manifested in various binaries: the European and African, the traditional and the modern, the native and the foreign, etc.[5] This aspect of both traditionalist and colonialist ideology is held in place by an essentializing connection between place and identity. Ironically, such dualism masks the link between traditionalism and colonialism since together they compose one of the primary binaries they both endorse. In fact, masking and simplifying divisions and connections is a key means by which binaries perpetuate neocolonialism, preventing a more nuanced understanding of oppression and exploitation. For example, binaries legitimate exploitative power structures within Sudan by suggesting that resistance entails both the conquest of the foreign and the reassertion of a pure cultural, national, and personal identity uninfected by the foreign. The language of infection, intimately tied to the language of traditionalism in Salih's novel, prevents recognition that the nation is exploited by elites within Sudan who are allied with European economic interests. (It should also be noted that the rhetoric of conquest, infection, and purity ends up playing itself out in the novel quite often on the bodies of women and through the ideologies of gender.)

In *Season of Migration,* the origins and development of neocolonialism are first traced in the character of Mustafa Sa'eed. Mustafa, born in the year of the British conquest of the Sudan (1898), is in every way the child of imperialism. With a dead father and a distant mother, he is subsumed by the colonial educational system when he is picked up and carried off to a colonial school by a colonial officer. (Yet he blindly continues to believe that entering school "was the first decision I had taken of my own free will" [21].) Because of his abilities, he quickly moves through this system and goes to England to finish his education. Despite his brilliance, however, he never considers how his education might have influenced his subsequent actions. After telling the narrator how he was first absorbed into the British school system, he remarks, "These events happened a long time ago. They are, as you'll now see, of no value" (21–22). Yet, the degree to which Mustafa's actions and motivations are shaped by his education is clearly reflected in his relations with women.

While in England, Mustafa wages a kind of imperial campaign against British women by seducing and discarding them. He sees his sexual conquests as a form of reverse colonization and as a means of anticolonial resistance, bragging "I, over and above everything else, am a colonizer" (94) and "I'll liberate Africa with my penis" (120). To entice the women, Mustafa mimics European stereotypes of Africa and the East. Speaking of one of these women, Isabella Seymour, Mustafa tells the narrator, "There came a moment when I felt I had been transformed in her eyes into a naked, primitive creature, a spear in one hand and arrows in the other, hunting elephants and lions in the jungles. This was fine" (38). Indeed, he not only permits, but actually encourages this vision of himself, telling Isabella, "'My face is Arab like the desert of the Empty Quarter, while my head is African and teems with a mischievous childishness" (38).

Mustafa's campaign reaches its frenzied culmination in his relationship with his British wife, Jean Morris. Both characters draw upon stereotypes of place to project aspects of their own personalities onto each other. For Mustafa, Jean is the cold north he wants to conquer, while for her he represents exotic Africa, identified as pure, mindless, destructive instinct. Of his desire for her, he says, "I was the invader who had come from the South, and this was the icy battlefield from which I would not make a safe return. I was the pirate sailor and Jean Morris the shore of destruction" (160). The ironic inaccuracy of such characterizations is revealed by the fact that Mustafa defines Jean as the icy north, even though he has repeatedly emphasized his own coldness. Their twisted relationship ends in her spurring him on to kill her during sex, as she cries, "Here are my ships, my darling, sailing towards the shores of destruction" (164). Mustafa's and Jean's words and actions manifest an imperial epistemic violence; because they define and separate identities based on place, they become an allegory of the objectifying and destructive colonial relationship. As the representation of colonial Europe, she lies to and steals from him; at one point she destroys his Sudanese cultural artifacts, promising him her body when she is done. This situation puts him in the bind of the colonized elite, trying to master the (for him) unattainable image of Europe; when he grows weary of the chase, she beckons him, promising that which she will never fully give: "When I avoided her she would entice me to her, and when I ran after her she fled from me" (156). He defines their relationship as a "murderous war in which no quarter was given" which "invariably ended" in his defeat (160). The outcome of their relationship suggests, however, that only mutual disaster can result from their Manichean epistemology: she succeeds in turning him into a murderous savage, the image of her own darkness, but in doing so she destroys herself.

Mustafa's relationships with British women and his perspective on these relationships also anticipates the connection, in the neocolonial state, between the rhetoric of resistance to a colonial other and the protection of power and exploitation. Mustafa's sexual campaign in no way weakens the structures of the colonial system. In fact, he strengthens them by perpetuating colonial binaries and stereotypes both in his characterization of the women he seduces and in his means of seduction, which entail his inhabiting the colonial image of the African. Yet he links these binaries and stereotypes with a rhetoric of resistance in order to justify his pursuit of his own pleasures and the damage he causes to others. This strategy connects Mustafa . with the postindependence Sudanese elites who use a rhetoric of resistance to imperial power to mask their concern "only with their stomachs and their sensual pleasures" (120). The connection between Mustafa and neocolonialism is made explicit when, after Mustafa's death, a minister at a conference tells the narrator that he was "a dear friend" of Mustafa's and that Mustafa was president of a society to which he belonged—"the Society for the Struggle for African Freedom" (120). Significantly, it is this man who tells the narrator that Mustafa said he would "liberate Africa" with his "penis." For Mustafa and those like him in the neocolonial racket, "the struggle for African freedom" is actually about the pursuit of their own desires and protection of their own interests. Mustafa is very much like Kurtz, who "lacked restraint in the gratification of his various lusts" (Conrad 57) and whose egoism is both perpetuated and masked by the rhetoric to which he subscribes. Mustafa also resembles the revolutionaries from *Under Western Eyes* who pursue their own greed and lust for power under the guise of abstract revolutionary rhetoric, and whose presence at the heart of the revolutionary movement suggests that a change in regime would by no means lead to a change in the horrors of Russian political structure and civil society.

Even after he has admitted, during his trial for Jean Morris' death, that he turned himself into a lie by allowing himself to embody the stereotype of the black African man, Mustafa continues to adhere to colonial notions of place. When he goes to the narrator's village after leaving England, he believes that he is entering a traditional world, kept pure from the cultural—although not the technological—influences of the modern and the European. He sees this move as an effort to expel or suppress the foreign within himself. His desire for cultural purity explains the layout of his home, in which he has divided the British part of his history (housed in a small, locked brick addition) from the rest of the traditional Sudanese house. He wants to keep his home and the village pure from the infection of modernity and European influence.

In actuality, the village is not at all the simple, pure place Mustafa imagines it to be. As Davidson points out, the sources of oppression in *Season of Migration* are not just rooted in colonialism; they are also to be found in certain aspects of traditional culture: "*Season* goes beyond a simple rejection of the European invasion and legacy. It offers a stunning critique of cultural segregationist moods by exposing in Sudanese culture the oppression that predated the British intrusion" (385). Nonetheless, in this novel, colonialism and traditionalism endorse a similar epistemology based on rigid binaries and boundaries. This epistemology is evident in the sad story of Mustafa's widow, Hosna. Three years after Mustafa apparently drowns himself in the Nile, Wad Rayyes, who is old, lecherous, and brutal, becomes obsessed with the idea of marrying Hosna. She does not want to marry him, but will be forced to because of the wishes of her family, which has complete control over her fate within patriarchal tradition. Like Mustafa, Wad Rayyes objectifies women in general—"Women and children are the adornment of life on this earth" (78)—and exoticizes foreign women: "Enough of you and your local girls. [. . .] The women abroad, they're the ones all right" (80–81). Both because she was married to the stranger Mustafa and because she embraces certain "modern" attitudes about gender relations, Hosna represents (for Wad Rayyes) the foreign element that he wishes to conquer; according to another villager, Mahjoub, "Even we who were her contemporaries and used to play with her in the village look at her today and see her as something new—like a city woman, if you know what I mean" (101). When the narrator refuses to marry Hosna himself, she is forced to marry Wad Rayyes against her will. When she refuses to sleep with Rayyes, he rapes her and she kills him and herself.

The connection between patriarchal traditionalism and colonialism is forcefully revealed in a crucial scene in which the narrator's grandfather tries to convince the narrator to be an intermediary between Wad Rayyes and Hosna. In the midst of his shock and anger, the narrator has a vision which connects Hosna with Mustafa's British victims:

The obscene pictures sprang simultaneously to my mind, and, to my extreme astonishment, the two pictures merged: I imagined Hosna Bint Mohammed, Mustafa Sa'eed's widow, as being the same woman in both instances: two white, wide-open thighs in London, and a woman groaning before dawn in an obscure village on a bend of the Nile under the weight of the aged Wad Rayyes. If that other thing was evil, this too was evil [. . .] (86–87)

This passage echoes one in *Heart of Darkness* from the scene in which Marlow meets Kurtz's Intended:

> I shall see this eloquent phantom [Kurtz] as long as I live and I shall see her too [the Intended], a tragic and familiar Shade resembling in this gesture another one [Kurtz's African Mistress], tragic also and bedecked with powerless charms, stretching bare brown arms over the glitter of the infernal stream. (75)

Viewed symbolically, this image suggests a parallel between European ideals (represented by the Intended) and a savage Africa in need of guidance (represented by the African mistress). In *Heart of Darkness,* both are betrayed by European imperialism, which promised to uphold and protect European ideals and bring them to "savage" Africa, but which actually focused on the satiation of greed and lust for power.

In Salih's novel, the scene has a slightly different resonance. The merging of the two women emphasizes the objectification of women and the focus on conquest and purity in both colonialist and traditionalist ideology. This link is suggested by the ironic resemblance of the two exploiters—Mustafa and Wad Rayyes—who represent, respectively, a colonial and traditional heritage. The parallels between the evils of colonialism and those found in traditionalism suggest the two are not as antithetical as the proponents of each would like to claim; as Aime Cesaire has said, European colonialism "has actually tended to prolong artificially the survival of local pasts in their most pernicious aspects" and in so doing "has grafted modern abuse onto ancient injustice, hateful racism onto old inequality" (179).

The village's response to the deaths of Hosna and Wad Rayyes reveals another similarity between traditionalism and colonialism. The village is in shock, but instead of questioning its patriarchal traditions, it absolves itself by blaming outside forces. As in colonialist ideology, all that is destructive and wrong is projected onto what is deemed foreign to the self. Thus, many of the villagers believe a root cause of the disaster was Hosna's "modern" notions. "What an impudent hussy! That's modern women for you!," says the narrator's mother (123). The narrator's grandfather, who used to laugh at Rayyes's brutal stories of his conquests, also blames the nature of women, saying, "God curse all women! Women are the sisters of the Devil. Wad Rayyes! Wad Rayyes!" (123). Mahjoub dismisses Wad Rayyes and Hosna as mad, without considering how that madness might have originated in the beliefs and actions of the village as a whole: "A mad man and a mad woman—how can we be to blame? What could we do about it?" (132) The implications of such a shifting of responsibility for neocolonialism are made explicit when a friend of the narrator's, "a young Sudanese who was lecturing at the University" says to an Englishman after independence, "You transmitted to us the disease of your capitalist economy. What did you give us except for a handful of capitalist companies that drew off our blood—and still do?" (60). While accurate in its critique of capitalism's effects, the Sudanese's accusation locates the blame for neocolonialism entirely outside of the speaker and Sudan and places it on external agents, assigning no responsibility to Sudanese sources of neocolonialism and to the Sudanese who benefit from it.

Yet, despite the notion of infection by the West, the incorporation of Western technology into the village is seen as beneficial. When he was young the narrator "saw the village slowly undergo a change: the water-wheels disappeared to be replaced on the bank of the Nile by pumps, each one doing the work of a hundred water-wheels" (4). He also notes the very architecture, the physical construction of the village, is changed as "iron doors" have replaced doors "fashioned from the wood of a whole tree" such as his grandfather's (70). In fact, the village is never identical with its past; it is always changing, just as the narrator's grandfather's stories change each time they are told, belying the narrator's belief in the grandfather's unchanging essence: "All these things [. . .] had their own histories which my grandfather had recounted to me time and time again, on each occasion omitting or adding something" (72–73).

The real issue, then, is not whether the village will change, but how it will change. The village traditionalists oppose any challenge to traditional structures of authority.[6] A wonderful (and horrible) image of this traditionalism is found in Mahjoub, one of the leaders of both the village and the local "National Democratic Socialist Party," who separates "a shoot from the mother date palm" and then throws the shoot "down to dry in the sun" (130–31). It is such (male) leaders, protecting their own power, who will decide which new shoots of village life will live and which will die. Modern technology is accepted; "modern women" are not.

In addition to showing how traditionalism works at the village level to protect power and prevent societal change, Salih reveals how it is linked with neocolonialism at the national level. The novel targets leaders who assume imperial privilege at the expense of the people, and who mask their actions by insisting Africa is endangered by an invasive disease of modern and foreign values. In this way, Salih echoes Fanon's and Ngugi's discussions of the deceptive use of nationalist, anti-European rhetoric by the native bourgeoisie. Recalling a conference on education he attended in Khartoum, the narrator describes the luxurious, European lifestyles of "the new rulers of Africa," and quotes from a speech in which the Minister of Education characterized modern values as an infection:

> Everyone who is educated today wants to sit at a comfortable desk under a fan and live in an air-conditioned house surrounded by a garden, coming and going in an American car as wide as the street. If we do not tear out this disease by the roots we shall have with us a bourgeois that is in no way connected with the reality of our life, which is more dangerous to the future of Africa than imperialism itself. (119–20)

Then the narrator points out that "this very man escapes during the summer months from Africa to his villa on Lake Lucerne" and that he has "created a vast fortune from the sweat dripping from the brows of wretched, half-naked people" (120). The minister's easy vilification of a bourgeois infected by foreign/modern values through education is revealed both as masking his and his cohorts' participation in neocolonialism, and a means of attacking potential competitors for its spoils ("everyone who is educated today"). In this way, Salih suggests not only how the villagers' beliefs are implicated in neocolonialism, but also how Fanon's own formulation of a clear split between the national bourgeoisie and the people can be used to reinforce the post-independence national configuration Fanon himself condemns. In *Season of Migration,* all rhetoric which enables the foisting of responsibility onto a foreign other is suspect.

The narrator himself is tied in numerous ways to the danger of neocolonialism primarily because, like Mustafa and the villagers, he assumes the rigid binaries of traditionalism and colonialism. When he returns from England, he thinks of the village as static and unitary, a cultural other to Europe unaffected by colonialism and modernity. And he sees himself as having an essential identity which is mirrored in the village. Thus, upon his return the narrator is comforted because he believes that he finds "the world as unchanged as ever" (2) and that he quickly gets back in touch with the essence of the village:

> it was not long before I felt as though a piece of ice were melting inside me, as though I were some frozen substance on which the sun had shone—that life warmth of the tribe which I had lost for a time in a land "whose fishes die of cold." (1)

This sense of rediscovery culminates in a belief that he finds himself reflected in the life of the village: "I was happy during those days, like a child that sees its face in the mirror for the first time" (4).

This notion of his identity leads the narrator to assert that, unlike Mustafa, his essential self remains untouched by (and apart from) his British education:

> Was it likely that what had happened to Mustafa Sa'eed could have happened to me? [. . .] I am from here—is not this reality enough? I too had lived with them [the British]. But I had lived with them superficially, neither loving nor hating them. (49)

Secure in the belief he is different from Mustafa, the narrator fails to recognize the symbolic significance of the fact that when he first enters Mustafa's secret British library, he momentarily mistakes a reflection of himself in a mirror for what he thinks is a picture of Mustafa: "It was my adversary Mustafa Sa'eed. The face grew a neck, the neck two shoulders [. . .] and I found myself standing face to face with myself" (135). The narrator's refusal to see how he might be similar to Mustafa prevents him from perceiving what they share: a neocolonial mindset shaped by colonial education and traditionalism. Here, Salih invokes the Conradian doubling relationship neither to write back to colonialism nor to make use of anticolonial elements in Conrad's texts, but to suggest the dangers of neocolonialism.

Blind to the ideological forces that control him, the narrator eventually becomes a tool of neocolonialism when he lands a job in Sudan's Ministry of Education. He and others like him in the ministry perpetuate the beliefs that prevent change and the Sudanese educational system thus serves the same function as under colonialism, albeit for a new set of masters. As the narrator tells Mahjoub, "Civil servants like me can't change anything. . . . If our masters say 'Do so-and-so, we do it'" (121).

In the course of the novel, the narrator's naivete is undermined by a series of destabilizing events. Early in the novel he refers to the villagers as "my people" (1), but after listening to Mustafa's story and observing what happens to Hosna, the narrator begins to question his prior sense of identification with the village: "There is no room for me here. Why don't I pack up and go? Nothing astonishes these people. They take everything in their stride. [. . .] They have learnt silence and patience from the river and from the trees. And I, what have I learnt?" (130) However, although the narrator revises his earlier sense of identification—now they are "these people"—he still homogenizes the village in terms of a stable, natural character; the difference is that now, while the village continues to represent the traditional, he represents the foreign and the modern and as a result no longer belongs there. There can be no mixing of categories, no instability of identity; he must remove himself so that both he and the village remain unitary.

It is not at all clear the narrator's naivete is ever entirely dispelled. Yet the end of the novel offers the possibility that the narrator takes another step in the process of growth and enlightenment and that this process may continue. In the ambiguous final scene, the narrator, who had been contemplating burning down Mustafa's British library, leaves the library after recalling Mustafa's account of his relationship with Jean, the English wife he eventually murdered. The memory of that story, focused on the dangers of projecting aspects of the self onto geographical others, inspires a change of heart: the narrator decides not to burn the library down. He seems to recognize the horrors he has witnessed will not be alleviated by purging the village of European cultural influences.

The narrator then goes to the Nile, plunges in, and begins to swim. In the middle of the river, in a kind of stupor, he almost drowns by allowing the power of the river to pull him down; but he revives and decides to live. After this symbolic rebirth, he acknowledges his former passivity—"All my life I had not chosen, had not decided"—and claims "duties to discharge" (168). One of these duties is evidently to tell his story, his last act within the pages of the novel. (The novel begins with the narrator telling his story to a group of "gentlemen" [1].) This notion of the duty of storytelling is anticipated through the positive influence of Mustafa's story on the narrator.

In contrast, silence is repeatedly connected in the novel with lack of reflection and a refusal to change. When an old friend of the narrator's grandfather, Bint Majzoub, tells the narrator the story of Hosna's and Wad Rayyes' deaths, she prefaces it by saying, "The things I'm going to say to you [. . .] you won't hear from a living soul in the village—they buried them with Bint Mahmoud and with poor Wad Rayyes" (125). The narrator decides it is his duty to tell the kind of story that the villagers wanted to bury—a story to challenge him and his audience by disrupting rigid and accepted ways of perceiving and organizing the world. This choice links the narrator with Marlow, who also decides to tell a story which disturbs him and his listeners, and hopefully undermine dangerous lies. For example, the story told by Marlow and the story told by Salih's narrator disrupt any positive images their audiences might have of the double figures and, more important, of the type of men the double figures represent. It is no more possible, after hearing the narrators' respective stories, to read Mustafa as a hopeful image of the postcolonial man who has mastered European civilization and can lead his own people out of colonialism, than it is to read Kurtz as a positive image of the colonial man going to save Africa with all his talents and superiority. In this regard, it is particularly interesting that Mrs. Robinson, Mustafa's surrogate English mother, aims to write a book praising his role in the anticolonial movement and clearing "his name of all suspicion" as a result of the trial (148). For the British, Mustafa is the perfect neocolonial figurehead, a man who could be manipulated even while remaining revered by his own people.[7]

Yet, the fact the narrator chooses to tell his story does not mean he understands its full significance, either for himself or his country. To him, Mustafa remains somewhat "like a genie who has been released from his prison and will continue thereafter to whisper in men's ears. To say what? I don't know" (55). The narrator's storytelling enables Mustafa to continue to "whisper," but the narrator clearly needs help in figuring out what is said. This may explain why the novel ends with his crying "Help! Help" in the water. If he needs help to be saved from the river, he also needs help in determining the significance of his story, and perhaps in creating a positive end for it. This can only happen if others also fight to understand, choose, and change.[8]

But who are these others? From whom is he looking for help and/or who is he trying to inform? There are some indications in the novel itself. When the narrator addresses his auditors as "gentlemen" and "Sirs," the implication is that the audience—although not necessarily the novel's— is male and has some authority. The auditors seem to be Arabic speakers, since the story is told in Arabic except when characters speak in English. It is likely, then, the narrator's target audience is those in power in Sudan—the very type of men who oppress and exploit their own land and people. This narrative frame constitutes another connection with *Heart of Darkness*. Marlow also tells his story to a group of male auditors—a "Director of Companies," a "Lawyer," an "Accountant"—who have authority and power in their society (7). However, there are important differences. Marlow asserts, "They—the women I mean—are out of it— should be out of it" (Conrad 49). Salih's narrator, in contrast, never suggests that women (and certain kinds of men) lack the necessary strength to understand and/or confront his story. In fact, the narrator frequently regrets that his own arrogance or cowardice prevents him from telling his and/or Mustafa's story to the villagers or to Hosna. It would seem that he chooses the "gentlemen" as his audience because *they* are the ones who most need to change if Sudan is to change.[9]

This discussion of the way Salih echoes the Conradian narrative structure and yet subtly departs from it brings us back to the issue of Salih's more general use and transformation of elements of Conrad's work in *Season of Migration to the North*. My analysis of the representation of postindependence neocolonialism in Salih's novel helps explain why Salih found Conrad's fiction so helpful in the pursuit of his own goals. Some of Conrad's most familiar narrative frameworks (especially those of *Heart of Darkness* and *Lord Jim*) emphasize the importance of storytelling and reflection in challenging fixed, ideologically determined constructions of the world. Such a challenge is precisely the aim of Salih's narrator. Conrad's tales of secret sharing are concerned with uncovering instances of covert and unrecognized complicity—for example between Kurtz and Marlow, or Leggatt and the young captain. *Season of Migration* emphasizes the shared responsibility for exploitation of those who seem to be polar opposites—for example, the aggressive Mustafa and passive narrator, the British educated Mustafa and the traditionalist Wad Rayyes. As Peter Nazareth notes, one of the useful aspects of Conrad's work for African writers in general is his "concept of the good guy *in* instead of *versus* the bad guy, contained in the very title 'The Secret Sharer,'" a concept that enables an attack on the colonialist worldview in which "Europeans could project their 'dark self' onto the 'dark people.'" ("Out" 218–19). Conrad's fiction also reveals that as long as people remain oblivious to the deeply embedded forces that control them, they will be unable to combat those forces. In *Under Western Eyes*, for example, most of the Russian characters are unaware of how their actions and thoughts are influenced by the autocracy which rules their lives. Betrayal is always the result of such unacknowledged control. Themes of control (by colonial and traditionalist ideology) and betrayal (of the postcolonial nation) are central in *Season of Migration to the North*. Given all these similarities, there is little doubt Conrad's usefulness for Salih goes far beyond the critical or complicit representations of colonialism and neocolonialism in Conrad's fiction. (This is not to say they are of no importance. Clearly, the representations of Belgian colonialism in *Heart of Darkness* and of neocolonialism in *Nostromo* are useful for Salih.)

Yet it is also true Salih transforms the significance of the Conradian elements in his story. For example, by emphasizing the importance of collective enlightenment, Salih rewrites the hierarchical, Conradian relationship—especially in *Heart of Darkness*—between a knowledgeable narrator and ignorant characters and auditors. Conrad's Marlow inscribes his knowledge and power through the course of his narrative by emphasizing what he (Marlow) knows and what his audience does not know, and by suggesting he has the strength to resist the call of the darkness:

> You can't understand? How could you [. . .] how can you imagine what particular region of the first ages a man's untrammeled feet may take him into by the way of solitude—utter solitude without a policeman—by the way of silence—utter silence, where no warning voice of a kind neighbor can be heard whispering of public opinion. These little things make all the great difference. When they are gone you must fall back upon you own innate strength, upon your own capacity for faithfulness. (49–50)

Salih's narrator, in contrast, consistently suggests the dangers of his naive sense of superiority to others, and his final call for help emphasizes the need for a collective production of knowledge and action. Without such communal production, he will remain essentially helpless and blind.[10] This may be why he remains without a name; his individual identity and development are not the final or central concern. In contrast, Conrad gives Marlow a name and makes his individual identity and development a primary focus.

Salih also rewrites Conradian conceptions of the link between landscape and identity. In *Heart of Darkness,* Africans are repeatedly described visually as part of the jungle. Such descriptions reflect Marlow's conception of them as unified with the chaotic, uncontrolled savagery of the African landscape, including the Congo river:

> But suddenly as we struggled round a bend there would be a glimpse of rush walls, of peaked grassroofs, a burst of yells, a whirl of black limbs, a mass of hands clapping, of feet stamping, of bodies swaying, of eyes rolling under the droop of heavy and motionless foliage. (37)

Similarly, the cultural and historical identity of the English is associated with the condition of the Thames river. Formerly, when the people were savage and bestial, the Thames was untamed and dangerous: "death skulking in the air, in the water, in the bush" (10). Now savagery is controlled, but by no means eliminated, by the "butcher and the policeman, in the holy terror of scandal and gallows and lunatic asylums" (49). As a result, Marlow proclaims: "We are accustomed to look upon the shackled form of a conquered monster, but there [along the Congo]—there you could look at a thing monstrous and free" (37). For the Africans the final implication of this link between place and race is that they could never offer an organized resistance or legitimate alternative to colonialism.[11]

In contrast, Salih represents those who assume an essential identity between people and landscape as being naive and dangerous. Mustafa and the women he seduces contribute to their own tragedies by identifying people with the heat of their native south or the cold of their native north. If the narrator initially accepts this conception of identity, then the narrative traces his growing awareness of the absurdity of an essential, natural link between character and place. While driving through the heat of the desert from the village to Khartoum, the narrator reflects: "How strange! How ironic! Just because a man has been created on the Equator some mad people regard him as a slave, others as a god" (108). At the end of the novel, the narrator completely rejects the relationship between identity and landscape. Throughout his story, he suggests he is rooted in the landscape of the village and this landscape has given him his identity. While in the river, he recognizes his true relationship with it:

> Then my mind cleared and my relationship to the river was determined. Though floating on the water, I was not part of it. I thought that if I died at that moment, I would have died as I was born—without any volition of mine. (168)

Not only does the narrator reject the link between his identity and the river, but he also connects his previous acceptance of this link with death and control. To accept the idea that landscape determines character and identity is to relinquish self-determination and endanger oneself. By challenging the connection between identity and landscape, the novel implies that, instead of assuming an essential commonality based on place and race, it is more fruitful to identify common interests as determined by struggle and oppression.

In the final analysis, despite the many similarities between Conrad's work, particularly *Heart of Darkness,* and *Season of Migration to the North,* there is a fundamental discontinuity between the goals and visions of Salih and Conrad. This is partly evident in the contrasts between the two authors, but it is also manifested in their dissimilar positions on irony, ignorance, and hope. Both Salih's novel and *Heart of Darkness* are rich in irony, but the sources of irony are crucially different. "The horror" at the center of *Heart of Darkness* threatens to corrode all truth, all ideals, and all bases for action. It creates the necessary and eternal Conradian irony defined by Emilia Gould in *Nostromo:* "There was something inherent in the necessities of successful action which carried with it the moral degradation of the idea" (431). This corrosive irony makes it possible for Marlow to defend his lie to the Intended. Because Marlow believes women are weaker than men and need their protection, he convinces himself and possibly his audience that the Intended would have been destroyed by the knowledge implicit in Kurtz's last words; he lies to keep the darkness "back alone for the salvation of another soul" (72). In Conrad's ironic world, it is necessary to lie, and thus to keep ignorant, in order to save. Marlow constructs this lie as an act of self-sacrifice since earlier in his narrative he tells his audience, "There is taint of death, a flavour of mortality in lies—which is exactly what I hate and detest in the world—what I want to forget" (29).

In contrast, in *Season of Migration to the North,* irony is a product of ignorance, and to perpetuate ignorance in others is to preclude necessary change. This means the condescending belief that others should be kept in ignorance because they could not understand or cope with the truth is necessarily destructive. For example, the narrator repeatedly wishes he had not been so arrogant as to believe Mahjoub could not understand the significance of what he experienced both in Britain and in the capital: "I did not say this to Mahjoub, though I wish I had done so, for he was intelligent; in my conceit I was afraid he would not understand" (3–4). In *Season of Migration to the North,* hope rests in part on the reduction of irony through storytelling and collective interpretation, and leads to effective action.

At the heart of Salih's novel is the narrator's cry for "Help," which is symbolically read as a plea for salvation from the neocolonial mindset through collective interpretation and action. The central ambiguity of the novel is whether or not the auditors and the readers will actually try to understand and act; in this sense, whether the novel is read as optimistic or pessimistic is determined outside of its pages. Yet the very possibility of optimism as a result of collective enlightenment and action is what distinguishes *Season of Migration to the North* from *Heart of Darkness;* at the heart of Conrad's novel is the "horror" which corrodes hope. It is the distance between "the horror" and "help" that defines the degree to which Salih has transformed the Conradian elements he has used.

4

Subjects in History

Disruptions of the Colonial in
Heart of Darkness and *July's People*

In 1982, Nadine Gordimer claimed that the fall of apartheid in South Africa, which she saw as imminent, would represent the end of one kind of colonialism: "It's inevitable that nineteenth-century colonialism should finally come to its end [in South Africa], because there it reached its ultimate expression" ("Living" 262). Faced with the destruction of the system that had determined colonial subjectivity, Gordimer suggested, whites would need to "redefine themselves in a new collective life within new structures" (264). This process would necessarily be difficult because the white subject, which "has always seen all of South Africa as ordered around it" (263), was constructed through the constant and invisible operation of the colonial system in the everyday; if whites were to change, they would need to rid themselves of a "hierarchy of perception that white institutions and living habits implant throughout daily experience in every white, from childhood" (265). A year earlier, Gordimer had vividly depicted in her novel *July's People* the imagined moment of the fall of apartheid and its effect on a white family forced to flee to their servant's village. This novel both represents the destabilizing of the white subject and its "hierarchy of perception" in a revolutionary present and suggests the way this subjectivity has been fully constructed and naturalized by the operation of colonial "institutions and living habits." The novel ultimately indicates that an effective and lasting disruption of the colonizer's identity will only be realized when there is a material challenge to or rejection of those "institutions and living habits."

This important point is given historical depth and brought into focus by an intertextual relationship between *July's People* and Conrad's *Heart of Darkness*. That relationship has largely been ignored, apart from a passing comment by Rosemarie Bodenheimer: "When Nadine Gordimer takes the Smales family to the South African bush in flight from a revolution they support, she deliberately invokes for the first time in her career the *Heart of Darkness* pattern of colonialist fiction" (108).[1] Bodenheimer, however, by no means does justice to the relationship between the novels. She claims that *July's People* invokes a "*pattern* of colonialist fiction," which *Heart of Darkness* metonymically represents (this description of Conrad's novel is itself extremely questionable), but the depth and nature of the connections between the novels suggest the significance of the intertextual relationship is less generic than Bodenheimer's formulation would indicate. In both novels, white protagonists travel into an African "wilderness" where they find that colonial categories and definitions, which they took to be real and natural, are challenged. This situation poses threats to the grounding for their subjectivity, which they struggle to affirm. Both texts, then, trace the vacillation of the protagonists between moments of doubt regarding the assumptions generated by colonial discourse and the reiteration of these assumptions in their attempts to ground their identities.

However, despite the general similarities between *July's People* and *Heart of Darkness,* the two novels diverge in terms of their settings and plots. Unlike Marlow, who takes a trip up the Congo during the heyday of European imperialism as an employee of one of the largest and most heinous imperial projects, Maureen Smales—Gordimer's protagonist— must go to live in the heart of the African wilderness and become dependent on those who live there precisely because the imperial system which determined her place in the world is in the process of being destroyed. These differences in circumstances result in important differences between the two protagonists in terms of the degree to which they are able to hold onto an ordering of the world determined by colonial discourse and to become aware of the operation of colonial discourse *as* discourse. Despite his exposure of the brutality of Belgian imperialism, as well as his questioning of colonial assumptions, Marlow often uses the representational economy of colonial discourse to reinforce his own authoritative identity. When he does so, he is not directly challenged by the perspective or voice of any character in his story or in his audience, and he is able to recuperate, at least in part, a colonial organization of the world. In *July's People,* Maureen is an "enlightened" liberal who is willing, up to a point, to examine her assumptions as they are brought into question by her experiences in July's village. However, she is not prepared to confront the constructed and contradictory nature of her identity, and she tries desperately to hold onto this identity. Unlike Marlow, Maureen is utterly unable to achieve this recuperation because of the transformation of her relationship with her servant July. As a result of this relationship, she is forced to confront the exposure and shattering of her colonial subjectivity and the assumptions on which it rests.

It is the particular configuration of similarities and differences between the two novels which makes the intertextual relationship between them so effective in clarifying and emphasizing the notion that any substantive, lasting disruption of colonial subjectivity can only occur when colonial roles and practices have been concretely undermined or rejected. Gordimer creates a protagonist who, much like Marlow, is willing to question many of the assumptions of colonial discourse, but who also continues to hold onto many of these same assumptions in order to maintain her identity. However, unlike Marlow, she is unable to avoid confronting a complete exposure and breakdown of the constructed nature of that identity because of a dramatic transformation of colonial roles. Thus, the combination of the similarity between Marlow's and Maureen's characters and the differences between their situations make clear how crucial the material stability or instability of colonial "institutions and living habits" is for the perpetuation or corrosion of colonial discourse and subjectivity.

It is also possible to read the intertextual relationship as reinforcing this point because that relationship serves to suggest the limitations of *Heart of Darkness* itself and the circumstantial causes for those limitations. The narrative structure of Conrad's novel, combined with Marlow's own skepticism about colonialism, might encourage the reader to interrogate and question the ways that Marlow perpetuates a colonial ordering of the world, but *Heart of Darkness* by no means offers a clear, alternative perspective or voice which would result in an unambiguous challenge to this ordering. Produced by a European author at a time when European imperial powers controlled most of Africa and colonial assumptions about Africa were widely held, Conrad's novel cannot envision a legitimate alternative way of representing and organizing the world that would completely undermine the categories and definitions of colonial discourse.[2] As a result, and despite its progressive vision, *Heart of Darkness* ultimately remains ambivalent in its rejection of this discourse. In contrast with Conrad's novel, *July's People* was produced in Africa when the era of direct white rule was about to end and written by an author who actively worked for the destruction of apartheid. These very different circumstances of production result in a novel which consistently and concretely presents means of organizing and representing the world that are utterly different from those bequeathed by colonial discourse and that mount a full, unmediated attack on the terms of that discourse. *July's People* suggests such an attack and the subsequent potential for a lasting disruption of colonial subjectivity rely on the disruption of subject positions determined by a colonial system. Given the fact that Gordimer's novel encourages an intertextual reading with *Heart of Darkness,* the difference between Gordimer's perspective and Conrad's (and the possible causes for this difference) gives concrete historical depth to this point.

One important implication of this contrapuntal reading[3] is that it suggests the disruptive potential in colonial discourse, which has been brilliantly outlined in many of Homi Bhabha's early essays, can only be realized in a lasting and meaningful way (rather than remaining contained) under specific material conditions. Bhabha's essays focus, in different ways, on the contradictions and conflicts at the very heart of colonial discourse that enable those who have been marginalized by colonialism to disrupt the authority and coherence of the colonizer's identity (whether intentionally or inadvertently). As we will see, both *Heart of Darkness* and *July's People* depict this potential in colonial discourse, and in this sense Bhabha is extremely useful for understanding how both novels can be read as undermining that discourse. However, in Conrad's novel the destabilization of colonial subjectivity is at least partially contained, while in Gordimer's it is fully realized. *July's People* would suggest this difference is a result of the circumstances of production of the novels, and as a result serves to emphasize what Bhabha's essays often do not—the central importance of sociopolitical factors for the successful debilitation of colonial subjectivity and authority.

After the past two decades of criticism on *Heart of Darkness,* it is difficult to deny Conrad's novel offers a perspective on colonialism and colonial discourse that is highly critical and insightful for the time.[4] Even Frances Singh, in her article on the novel's "colonialist bias," claims *Heart of Darkness* is "one of the most powerful indictments of colonialism ever written" (268). Despite Marlow's often explicit colonialist bias, his own skepticism is the most obvious means by which Conrad achieves this indictment. As Andrea White argues, Marlow challenges the assumptions of both his listeners aboard the Nellie and the nineteenth-century reader, especially by subverting the expectations set up by the colonialist adven-

ture story: "Marlow's combative and challenging relationship to the frame
he occupies and the events he narrates works to dislodge the myth kept in
place by the dominant fiction" (178). Most obviously, of course, Marlow
punctures the myth of the civilizing mission in the Congo, revealing both
the cruelty and rapacity of Belgian imperialism and its use of colonial
rhetoric to mask its abuses. However, he also brings into question the
moral foundations of imperialism in general. Before beginning his story
he proclaims, "The conquest of the earth, which mostly means the taking
it away from those who have a different complexion or slightly flatter
noses than ourselves, is not a pretty thing when you look into it too
much" (10). If he goes on to claim it can be redeemed by "an idea at the
back of it," the fact one needs "an unselfish belief" in this idea—given the
rest of the narrative's unsparingly critical take on all motives *and* abstract
ideas—suggests Marlow's skeptical approach to the issue. As White notes,
this skepticism is particularly apparent in his dialogic challenge to the
simplistic nationalist and imperialist views of the first narrator (186).

Marlow's questioning of assumptions generated by colonial discourse
also includes his problemitizing of easy and clear distinctions between
Europeans and Africans. These distinctions are the underpinnings for
both colonial identities and the rigid hierarchies which justify colonialism. Repeatedly, Marlow suggests his experience in Africa made him realize there are no essential ethical or spiritual differences between the colonizer and the colonized. With this suggestion, he is challenging his
audience's belief that they automatically have the obligation and right to
conquer and rule other peoples. Although the similarity he articulates is
often negative because he suggests Europeans and Africans are linked by
a savage, instinctual human nature, he does suggest, if only briefly, that
Africans, like Europeans, have their own culture which is not simply
another sign of their primal, degenerate condition. Thus, as Abdul Jan-
Mohamed notes, Marlow's equation between "the function of African
drumming with that of church bells in a Christian country" can be read
as a rejection of "the traditional colonialist use of drumming as the
emblem of the natives' evil" (90). At one point, when Marlow observes "a
bit of white worsted" around a native's neck, he even gestures towards the
possibility that the Africans could assimilate manufactured European
objects into their own symbolic system: "Was it a badge—an ornament—
a charm—a propitiatory act?" (21). As Bhabha notes, "Marlow interrogates the odd, inappropriate, 'colonial' transformation of a textile into an
uncertain textual sign, possibly a fetish" (105). Bhabha uses this moment
in *Heart of Darkness* as an example of his notion of the hybrid which

involves the use of symbols from the west in ways other than they were intended and for unexpected purposes, leading to the destabilizing of the meaning of the symbol and the colonizer's control over that meaning. Marlow may not follow through with the implication of the hybrid object he observes for colonial discourse, but he at least is willing to acknowledge the possibility that Africans could achieve a symbolic transformation of European objects.

However, Marlow also perpetuates colonial conceptions of otherness, which not only underpin the racial hierarchies that legitimize colonialism but are also a key component of his own (authoritative) identity. Chinua Achebe focuses on this aspect of the narration in "An Image of Africa" (where he equates it with the perspective of the novel as a whole). For Achebe, Marlow's "advanced and humane views" are those of a "kind of liberalism" which "required all Englishmen of decency to be deeply shocked by atrocities in Bulgaria or the Congo" but which also "managed to sidestep the ultimate question of equality between the white people and black people" (256). (As we will see, such liberalism is an important similarity between Marlow and Gordimer's protagonist Maureen Smales, as well as a primary political target of *July's People*.) Although Marlow frequently admits his own lack of understanding of the Africans and their behavior, his inability to comprehend is usually represented as resulting from the Africans' absolutely primal condition (which, as Singh notes, comes to be equated with "evil" and "spiritual darkness" [271]). In a passage Achebe quotes at length, Marlow proclaims he and the other Europeans "could not understand" the Africans dancing on the shore because they are "prehistoric," "from the night of first ages, of those ages that are gone" (37). In tune with this suggestion, Marlow claims the similarity between Europeans and Africans can only be understood in terms of a lowest common denominator. All humans have a bestial, instinctive nature which is found in its purest form amongst the Africans: "What thrilled you was just the thought of their humanity—like yours—the thought of your remote kinship with this wild and passionate uproar. Ugly" (38). Thus, despite his doubts, Marlow often remains loyal to colonial stereotypes; Africans are part of the primeval condition that is Africa, and the problem with Kurtz is that he went native by becoming part of this condition. As Achebe notes, Kurtz becomes "a wayward child of civilization who willfully had given his soul to the powers of darkness and 'taken a high seat amongst the devils of the land'" (256).

This construction of Africa and Africans enables Marlow to maintain an authoritative colonial identity for himself and, possibly, for other British men. If Africans are part of the primal condition that Africa represents, then they necessarily lack the ability to restrain the darkness. Therefore, Europeans capable of resisting their own primal selves in Africa and of teaching such resistance to Africans deserve the authority bequeathed the colonizer by colonialism. Marlow subtly suggests he is one such European. He does not go ashore "for a howl and a dance" (38), despite the strong temptation, and he uses his position of authority to prevent the Africans from giving into their temptations. For example, the fireman "ought to have been clapping his hands and stamping his feet on the bank, instead of which he was hard at work" (38–39), but this is only because Marlow has frightened him: "He was useful because he had been instructed; and what he knew was this—that should the water in that transparent thing disappear the evil spirit inside the boiler would get angry through the greatness of his thirst and take a terrible vengeance" (39). In this way, Marlow suggests that he is one of those British men who make the "vast amount of red" on the colonial map of Africa "good to see at any time because one knows that some real work is done in there" (13).[5] In this construction of African and European identities, Africa becomes the embodiment of that within the European self which must be contained in order for that self both to remain European—once one has left the confines of Europe—and to do the work of "civilizing" which legitimates colonial authority. Marlow's insight, that there is not a necessary and absolute separation between Europe and Africa, actually ends up allowing him to reinscribe his own (colonial) identity and authority in the narrative. He suggests that by first resisting the darkness within himself and then combating the darkness in Africa, he has proven his difference from the Africans and the Belgians.

Marlow is greatly aided in this construction of identity by the actual authority he wields over Africans and by the fact he never interacts with them in ways that are not determined by the roles and practices bequeathed by colonialism. He commands and directs his crew and they remain means to his ends. As a result, it is all too easy for him to represent them as becoming useful and improved as a result of his intervention. Furthermore, when Marlow comments on Africans and their behavior, he does so from the position of the colonial observer, who assumes the ability to interpret and ascribe meaning to Africans and their behavior. This dynamic necessarily serves to reinforce colonial conceptions of identity and hierarchy. As Paul Armstrong points out,

> Marlow remains for the most part an observer who does not communicate with the objects of his observation [. . .] he remains

a tourist who sees the passing landscape through a window which separates him from it, and he consequently commits the crimes of touristic misappropriations of otherness. (24–25)

It can, of course, be argued the novel itself undermines Marlow's efforts to continue to place Africa in a colonial narrative and, thereby, to stabilize his identity. As Sarvan notes, the text "separates author from character" (282) and holds the potential to disrupt Marlow's efforts to contain the significance of what he has seen and told. The quotation marks around every utterance of Marlow's, his faltering, convoluted, and contradictory attempts to make sense of his experience, the degree to which his story brings into question the smug first narrator's notion of Britain's relationship with the world, all remind the reader that Marlow's story too is a construct to be questioned and analyzed—a necessarily inadequate attempt to make sense of his experiences. As Edward Said has written:

> Conrad's self-consciously circular narrative forms draw attention to themselves as artificial constructions, encouraging us to sense the potential of a reality that seemed inaccessible to imperialism, just beyond its control [. . .] Conrad's way of demonstrating [the] discrepancy between the orthodox and his own views of empire is to keep drawing attention to how ideas and values are constructed (and deconstructed) through dislocations in the narrator's language. (28–29)[6]

In other words, reading *Heart of Darkness* in the deconstructive way Said claims the text itself encourages enables the reader to uncover the contradictions and silences of colonial discourse that Marlow represses and that threaten to undermine—even more completely than he does—the identities and authority constructed by colonial discourse.

A good example of the usefulness of this approach to Marlow's narrative involves the well-known moment when he describes the African fireman, who has been trained to use technology, as "a dog in a parody of breeches and a feather hat walking on his hind legs" (38). This moment stages the threat to colonial subjectivity represented, in Homi Bhabha's terms, by mimicry. The disruptive form of colonial mimicry develops because, while colonialism encourages the colonized to emulate the colonizer, to become mimic men, the colonized cannot *be* the colonizer because this would disrupt the legitimacy of the hierarchical colonial relationship. Thus, we have the now well-known concept of "not quite/not white" (92). As Bhabha suggests, this construction potentially creates a fracturing image that mocks the colonizer and resists his or her control; the familiar is transformed and mastery is undone. If one reads Marlow's comment (about the fireman) against the grain, and in terms of this concept of mimicry, then his expression of open, brutal racism, an anomaly in the narrative as a whole, is seen as a sign of his own discomfort with the implications of what he has depicted. The image of an African blurring the distinction between African and European in such a fundamental way exacerbates Marlow's anxiety and results in his attempt to create an absolute gulf between himself and the fireman by suggesting the latter is of a different species. Because of Marlow's vitriol in this scene, a skeptical approach to his narration has the potential to make apparent an underlying disruptive contradiction at the heart of colonial discourse in a more vivid way than could be achieved by any direct articulation of it.

Yet, as Said points out, if Conrad had a skeptical view of imperialism and, through his narrative style, indirectly enabled a potentially corrosive examination of colonial discourse, he still subscribed to certain underlying assumptions generated by that discourse:

> Conrad could probably never have used Marlow to present anything other than an imperialist world-view, given what was available for either Conrad or Marlow to see of the non-European at the time. Independence was for whites and Europeans; the lesser or subject peoples were to be ruled; science, learning, history emanated from the West. True, Conrad scrupulously recorded the differences between the disgraces of Belgian and British colonial attitudes, but he could only imagine the world carved up into one or another Western sphere of domination. (24)

Said's reference here to the kind of representations of the non-European that would have been available to Conrad is extremely important because it points to the way the imperial system, at its height, placed limits on what could be imagined and understood by Europeans and as a result on the degree to which colonial discourse itself could be exposed as a construct. *Heart of Darkness* does not present an alternative perspective from the other side of empire which would offer a truly alternative ordering of the world. As a result, it may gesture towards the contradictions and silences of colonial discourse and the constructed nature of colonial subjectivity, but its attack remains circumscribed. This may be why the predominant

judgment in the last twenty years of criticism (since Achebe's condemnation of Conrad), is that *Heart of Darkness* has a profoundly ambivalent
relationship with colonialism and colonial discourse.[7]

July's People suggests that an inability to break from the conception of
the world generated by colonial discourse, even for as anticolonial writer
as Conrad, is the necessary result of continuing to live within colonial
political and social structures. Gordimer's protagonist, Maureen Smales, is
a liberal who has been critical of apartheid policy; yet, the novel reveals
how utterly her identity and perspective have been formed by apartheid
institutions and practices and how her continued participation in a colonial social order prevented her from ever really interrogating her most fundamental assumptions. In this sense, Maureen's liberalism is very similar to
Marlow's (at least as it is described by Achebe). Only as the colonial order
breaks down and habitual roles are transformed is she forced to become
aware of and to question all the fundamental underpinnings of her reality.
In particular, this disruption is the result of the transformation of the master-servant relationship between July and Maureen, which enables him to
break from the restrictions imposed on his actions and speech by his role
as servant. Despite the fact that Maureen sees herself as having an open
mind, as the novel progresses she becomes an increasingly unwilling par-
ticipant in the process of her own enlightenment. Once she finds the
grounding for her identity undermined by July, she tries desperately to
recuperate it, but he continues to challenge her. As a result, her identity
becomes increasingly unstable, and she becomes steadily more trauma-
tized. The important difference between Marlow and Maureen is that she
is not able to successfully affirm her identity and the colonial assumptions
on which it depends because, in the wake of an armed revolt, the colonial
other is able to articulate his perspective and challenge her own.

The beginning of *July's People* signals its intertextual relationship with
Heart of Darkness through its references to a voyage into the African landscape, which also becomes a movement into the self and towards enlightenment. In echoes of Marlow's river journey, the vehicle which takes the
Smales to July's village, the bakkie, is even referred to figuratively as a
"ship" (14). However, unlike in *Heart of Darkness,* the voyage itself is not
important; it is short and leaves little time for reflection, even while it
takes the Smales family into a world that shatters the limits of Conrad's
cognitive landscape. When the novel begins with the Smales waking up
in an African hut, they are already (figuratively) beyond Marlow's furthest
point of navigation and about to embark on an interior journey that neither they nor Conrad could ever have imagined.

As the novel opens, the reader is immediately made aware of the way that Maureen's unexpected situation is already transforming her reality. When July comes to give the Smales breakfast on their first morning in his village, there is a continued acting out of their traditional relationship: "You like to have some tea?—July bent at the doorway and began that day for them as his kind has always done for their kind." The use of the term kind here—suggesting some kind of biological categorization—points to the degree to which July's position vis-à-vis the Smales has been naturalized in South Africa.[8] This naturalization has masked the way that apartheid has determined the conditions of subservience imposed on July's "kind." With that system under attack, the relations between July and the Smales begin to modify. This is first signaled by the change in place for the Smales. Usually the morning service would begin with "the knock on the door," but here there is "no door" only "an aperture in thick mud walls" (1). In turn, this lack of a knock is a silent reminder that the relationship with July has changed. In his village, they are now dependent on him in a way that they have not been before; he is not just their servant but also their "host." The unimaginable transformation of circumstances results in the beginnings of Maureen's awareness of the limitations of her colonial construction of the world. After only a few days in the village, when she tries to read a novel, she discovers she cannot because "the false awareness of being within another time, place, and life that was the pleasure of reading, for her, was not possible. She was in another time, place, consciousness. [. . .] No fiction could compete with what she was finding she did not know, could not have imagined or discovered through the imagination" (29). Maureen's new position necessitates that she confronts a "time, place, and consciousness" that has not been mapped by colonial discourse and which lie, as a result, beyond her "imagination." In this way, her situation is similar to Marlow's in that he too was forced to confront that which exceeded colonial constructions of reality and the limits of his own imagination (for example, the cannibles inexplicable "restraint" in not eating the European "pilgrims" [43]).

However, despite the shift in positions, a perpetuation of the master-servant relationship initially enables Maureen to hold onto her construction of July and herself. At first, July acts as their servant in his village—for example by serving them breakfast—and they continue to expect him to take care of them and their things. Maureen's husband Bam even expects July to assist him in rigging up a water tank in the village in the same way that they have always worked together; Bam does the conceptual and organizational work,

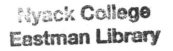

while July is his helper. The repetition of this dynamic—the same dynamic which exists between Marlow and his crew—perpetuates the Smales' notion of who has the proper knowledge and skills to lead and direct. Even though July has shown his ability to supervise, provide, and lead in their journey to his village (by directing them hundreds of miles under dangerous circumstances and by securing gas), he remains in the same category as Marlow's helmsman, "a help—an instrument" whose deficiencies need to be "worried about" and monitored (*Heart* 51). This conception of July is enabled by his own initial acceptance of the habitual roles determined by apartheid, as he fails to recognize the Smales' dependency. It is worth noting the novel repeatedly indicates that July's subjectivity has *also* been shaped by apartheid.[9]

The fact that Maureen has not let go of a colonial representation of the world is also reflected in the way she continues to conceive of the village. In the past, she understood township and homeland life in terms of the exoticizing perspective of "a natural history museum" (24) and "photographic exhibitions" in a "suburban mall" (125). This perspective both categorizes South Africa's black majority as primitive and perpetuates the sense of an essential disjunction between the conditions under which that majority lives and the "modernity" of which she is a part. At first, Maureen represents the village in these terms. It is, just like Marlow's Congo, absolutely and necessarily premodern—a place where technology does not naturally belong. Thus, when she sees "very small mirrors" dangling in a hut, the presence of "something intricately banal, manufactured, replicated, made her turn as if someone had spoken to her from back there" (29). Similarly, the bakkie is "a ship that had docked in a far country. Anchored in the khakiweed, it would rust and be stripped to hulk, unless it made the journey back, soon" (14).[10]

However, the novel makes it abundantly clear the village is by no means outside of the modern; it has been predominately shaped by the apartheid system, and this process has necessarily included its assimilation of technology.[11] At the same time, because of its positioning within apartheid and its subsequent poverty and because of the impact of cultural practices which predate colonization, the village's use of both technologically manufactured items and technology itself is alien to Maureen and her family: "battered hub-caps salvaged from wrecked cars" become part of a "pig-pen" (28); "a car seat" becomes part of the reception area for a chief (114); and "zinc finials [. . .] for those who could afford them, had replaced the cone of mud packed on the apex of roofs" (137). The "Gumba-Gumba" man is a particularly interesting example of the village's cultural economy. The term, Gumba-Gumba, comes from "the village people's language" and reflects a concept unknown to Maureen and her family:

> The red box was the area's equivalent of a traveling entertainment; someone had brought back from the mines a battery-operated amplifier and apparently he would come and set it up in this village or that, attached to a record player, for an occasion. It was not clear what this occasion was. (140)

By using "white" technology for an unexpected and previously unknown purpose, the Gumba-Gumba man creates a hybrid object—like Conrad's "white worsted"—which challenges the rigid categories and identities of colonial discourse and, as a result, has the potential to disrupt it. However, if the hybridity of that white worsted in *Heart of Darkness*—the unknown and alien use of a manufactured product by Africans—creates a link between Conrad's novel and Gordimer's, the sheer number of such hybrid objects and their kind in *July's People* marks a significant difference between the two texts.

Maureen eventually begins to understand how fundamentally her own consciousness, and July's, has been shaped by apartheid. But it is significant that an interrogation of her most deeply held assumptions happens only after July takes the bakkie for the first time without asking permission. Up to this point, this action is the most important sign of the change in positions of power brought about by the disintegration of the old system. July takes action on his own, ownership of the vehicle is brought into question, and Maureen is made viscerally aware of her family's helplessness. Just days later, this overt transformation of roles leads Maureen to reflect more deeply than she has on July's existence as a gendered being, perhaps because for the first time she has seen him in the "male" role of provider and decision-maker. In turn, the break from her habitual way of seeing and understanding results in a critical re-evaluation of it.

Thinking about July's relationship with his "town woman," his mistress while he was in Johannesburg, Maureen thinks to herself, "Did he love the town woman? [. . .] And did that mean he would have liked to bring the town woman here and live with her permanently?" (64) But then she realizes his entire conception of love and its significance would be different from her own because of his place in the apartheid economic system. July has been forced to work in Johannesburg as a result of that system; only infrequently has he been able to return to his village. As a result, he has had to live two entirely and necessarily separate lives in a way she could never conceive of:

> "We" [whites] [. . .] understand the sacred power and rights of sexual love as formulated in master bedrooms, and motels with false names in the register. Here, the sacred power and rights of sexual love are as formulated in a wife's hut and a backyard room in a city. The balance between desire and duty is—has to be—maintained quite differently in accordance with the differences in the lovers' place in the economy. These alter the way of dealing with the experience; and so the experience itself. The *absolute nature* she and her kind were scrupulously just in granting to everybody was no more than the price of the master bedroom and the clandestine hotel tariff. (64–65)

If before, as a liberal (one of her "kind"), she extended a universal humanity to blacks and challenged certain overtly racist assumptions, she now must confront the fact that her notions of the most universal aspects of human experience—such as love and death—are a product of her position in the apartheid system and are necessarily different from July's. At the same time, she recognizes that her assumption of the "absolute nature" of her reality was generated by her privileged place within apartheid. In other words, the transformation of Maureen's relationship with July encourages her to move well beyond her former liberalism. She now critically explores her former perception of the world and the way that perception has been constructed.

Although Marlow also interrogates his habitual ways of seeing the world, it seems that at this moment Maureen outstrips him in terms of the clarity and extent of her epiphany. Yet, even after this potentially transformative realization, Maureen remains fundamentally similar to Marlow in her attempt to recuperate her colonial subjectivity in the face of all internal and external challenges to it. If in a moment of detached reflection she is willing and able to recognize the lack of authority and universality in her conceptions of human nature, she is still not prepared to systematically question and alter her identity. Unlike Marlow, however, she is left with no choice. As a result of the reversal of positions—marked by the Smales' dispossession of the bakkie and the gun—July for the first time feels able to confront Maureen with his point of view on their relationship. The subsequent revelations undermine Maureen's sense of a known, coherent self and ultimately make recuperation of that self impossible. Maureen responds to this fundamental threat to her sense of self with fear and aggression. Ironically, this response only serves to starkly expose the absence of the unitary identity she has always taken for granted.

In the first direct confrontation between them, July exposes a contradiction that has been suppressed between Maureen's position as July's "mistress" and her idea of herself as a progressive liberal. She believes she treated him as a man, "the word [boy] was never used in *her* house," but he asserts he was always only her servant, her "boy" (70). To prove his point, July asserts that Maureen believed he always had to be watched and directed in his duties around the house (like a child), and that she did not take account of the existence of an identity that would deviate from his role as servant: "But you, you don't think about me, I'm big man, I know for myself what I must do. I'm not thinking all the time for your things, your dog, your cat" (71). July undermines Maureen's sense of identity by revealing to her that, despite her liberal myth of herself, the relationship between them was only about economic exploitation—a relationship of servant and master. In this sense, he is enacting what Bhabha refers to as "the native's refusal to satisfy the colonizer's narrative demand" (99). As a result of a splitting found in colonial discourse in which the colonizer is *both* democrat, preparing the backward races for freedom and democracy, *and* despot, necessarily exercising complete control over those races, there is a threat of the fragmentation of colonial identity. According to Bhabha, this threat results in the "narcissistic colonialist demand [. . .] that the Other should authorize the self, recognize its priority, fulfil its outlines, replete, indeed, repeat, its references and still its fractured gaze" (98). However, when this narcissistic demand is refused there is a disruption of the colonial ego. This is precisely what happens to Maureen the first time July feels free to express his perspective on their relationship. In contrast, Marlow never has to face an overt and direct challenge to his construction of identity from one of his listeners (or, apparently, from any of the characters in his story); in fact, it is he that is challenging the assumptions of the other men aboard the *Nellie*.

In response to July's challenge, Maureen tries both to attack his conception of himself as a man who fulfills important responsibilities to others and to threaten him with the knowledge of his mistress whom he left behind and who may need his help: "If all you can think about is what happened back there, what about Ellen? [. . .] What is happening to Ellen? [. . .] Where is she in the fighting there? Has she got something to eat, somewhere to sleep? You were so concerned about your wife—and what does she think about Ellen?" (72) This aggressive response suggests a lack of positive, constructive adaptation to the new circumstances. In fact, in one sense, there is a return to the scene of direct colonial antagonism, what is referred to in the novel as "an archtypal sensation [. . .] like the swelling resistance of a vein into which a hollow needle is surging a substance in counterflow to the life-blood coursing there" (62).

Maureen comes to feel ever more threatened by July as he takes open possession of the bakkie and asserts his newfound authority and ability to speak openly. She is not afraid he is going to physically harm her or her family, but she is terrified by the control over their fates he now wields and by the continued threat he represents to her identity. In their second conflict, she becomes consciously aware of this fear: "It echoed no experience she had ever had. [. . .] She had never been afraid of a man. Now comes fear. [. . .] It spread from him" (98). This sense of threat intensifies in their final scene of conflict, after the Smales's shotgun has been taken.

In this final confrontation, Maureen initially lashes out at July by telling him she is "ashamed" he stole small things from her house. July strikes back by speaking in his own language which Maureen does not know:

> She understood although she knew no word. Understood every-
> thing: what he had had to be, how she had covered up to herself
> for him, in order for him to be her idea of him. But for himself—
> to be intelligent, honest, dignified for her was nothing; his mea-
> sure as a man was taken elsewhere and by others. She was not his
> mother, his wife, his sister, his friend, his people. (152)

The changes brought on by revolution—what Maureen earlier defines as "an explosion of roles" (117)—result in her recognition that he has always constructed identity and meaning in ways that escape and challenge her own representational authority. More specifically, July's use of his own language in response to Maureen's attempt to define him suggests to her the existence of a self that was defined "elsewhere and by others" in this language and that was never taken into consideration in the language of his servitude, described earlier as "the English learned in kitchens, factories, and mines" which "was based on orders and responses, not the exchange of ideas and feelings" (96). She also recognizes that the system, and her position in it, enables her to believe in the truth of "her idea of him"; for example, he had to play along with this idea because of economic necessity. This moment necessarily undermines Maureen's identity,

since she—in classic colonial fashion—has constructed herself as having
the ability (and therefore the right) to represent July. Repeatedly we are
told she has always believed "she was the one who understood him, the
way he expressed himself" (61).

Unable to respond constructively to the implications of her epiphany,
Maureen fruitlessly tries to attack and define July. However, in her fury
she reveals all the more clearly her loss of authority and identity, not only
because of the appearance of a previously unknown aggressive self but also
because, as David Spurr notes, the intensity with which the colonizer
affirms authority "increases as [this] authority loses its grasp" (124):

> Steal a bakkie. You want that now. [. . .] You want the bakkie, to
> drive around in like a gangster, imagining yourself a *big man*,
> important, until you don't have any money for petrol, there isn't
> any place to buy, and it'll lie there, July, under the trees, in this
> place among the old huts, and it'll fall to pieces while the chil-
> dren play in it. Useless. Another wreck like all the others.
> Another bit of rubbish. (153)

Returning once again to the categories and hierarchies determined by
colonial discourse, Maureen challenges July's ability to make use of and
master technology and, concomitantly, his right to the authority which
such mastery entails. Despite evidence to the contrary, she insists the
bakkie will become "useless" and his belief that he is a "big man" will be
exposed as a sham. Furthermore, in order to suggest that July has *improp-
erly* usurped the Smales' authority, as marked by possession of the bakkie,
Maureen asserts he has stolen it, even though the circumstances of the
Smales' dispossession is drastically misrepresented by this term.

This final, fruitless attempt to hold onto colonial identities, which
have become obsolete, and Maureen's powerless and empty vehemence
reveal what has become increasingly obvious throughout the narrative:
she remains unable to adapt to and cope productively with the transformation of roles entailed by revolutionary political circumstances. In the
context of the novel, this inability is the result of Maureen's interpellation
as a white South African by colonial institutions. The novel suggests Maureen's authority under apartheid makes it almost impossible for her to
adapt constructively to new configurations of power when that system is
destroyed. This debilitating limitation is, of course, in part caused by the
difficulty of giving up an authority which she was not even fully aware she
possessed. However, it also results from the fact that under apartheid

Maureen, unlike July, never had to acknowledge or accommodate ways of organizing and defining the world other than her own. This aspect of white, South African consciousness is emphasized when the narrator explains July is amused "to be the mentor" when the Smales try to grasp the social structure of July's home, "as if he didn't take too seriously a white's wish to comprehend or faculty of comprehension for what he [a white] had never needed to know as [in the way that] a black had the necessity to understand, take on, the white people's laws and ways" (112).

The notion that there could be significant and inescapable cognitive limitations imposed on whites by apartheid may explain why Gordimer said in 1982, "we whites have still to thrust the spade under the roots of our lives" ("Living" 271). Because white colonial subjectivity lacks adaptability, and in order for the white subject to prepare to deal constructively with systemic change, habitual roles must be dislocated. It is not enough to be a liberal and question the morality of the colonial system; one must "thrust the spade under the roots" of one's life. In other words, *July's People*'s dramatizes the limitations of a liberal approach to colonialism that is divorced from material social change.

Not surprisingly, given Maureen's inability to adapt, the novel ends with her complete psychological break down. In absolute terror, she instinctively runs towards a helicopter which has landed in the bush on the other side of the stream from the village. She does not know if she is running toward rebels, foreigners, or soldiers from the apartheid regime, and the result of this run remains indeterminate, since the novel ends before she reaches the helicopter. As some critics note, through its imagery, the ending does offer the possibility Maureen could be reborn as part of a new South Africa (Brink 175; Temple-Thurston 57). However, if there is a possibility of rebirth, it is not the result of a "choice" by Maureen to shed her old, useless identity and "run towards the future," as Andre Brink has suggested (176);[12] Maureen experiences a breakdown of her subjectivity and cannot, therefore, make a choice. She begins running because of an uncontrollable fear that overwhelms her: "Then she stands for a moment while fear climbs her hand-over-hand to throttle, hold her" (159). And the final passage depicts her as regressing to an unthinking, animal state: "She runs [. . .] alert, like a solitary animal at the season when animals neither seek a mate nor take care of young, existing only for their lone survival, the enemy of all that would make claims of responsibility" (160). Given these passages, it is difficult to argue Maureen consciously decides to reject the past and run towards a future. Furthermore, this description has been anticipated in a progression of images that suggest Maureen has become increasingly animal-like. Her children are referred to as "her litter" (47); she is described like a monkey who "scratched efficiently at her ribs" (89); and when the gun is taken, and the children look to her for comfort, "they knew, as they had learnt when a dog or cat was going to repulse them, that to touch was forbidden them" (145). After Maureen's final regression, the novel concludes with her literally disappearing into the natural scene as "she runs" (160). This moment, perhaps more than any other in the novel, links Gordimer's novel with Conrad's, since Maureen has become Kurtzian in her apparent loss of self and unification with the wilderness. However, this moment of connection also marks a departure. *July's People* in no way suggests Maureen's regression is the result of a capitulation to a primal interior darkness symbolized by a primordial and uncivilized Africa, as Marlow suggests about Kurtz. Instead, the novel makes it abundantly clear her heart of darkness is a "white" subjectivity constructed by the South African colonial system. Her interpellation by this system creates not only the contradictions and gaps that when exposed utterly disrupt the grounding for her identity, but also her inability to transform her identity to meet new political conditions.

Perhaps even more important, if in *Heart of Darkness* Marlow repeatedly suggests Africa itself has drawn out Kurtz's interior darkness and led to his surrender to it, *July's People* makes clear the darkness at the core of Maureen's identity has been uncovered and activated by the material destabilization of the institutions and structures of apartheid. In this way, Gordimer's novel has the potential to reveal the importance of political and social circumstances for the realization of the disruptive potential at the heart of colonial subjectivity. This point is sharpened by *July's People's* intertextual relationship with Conrad's novella. While both texts reinforce Bhabha's perception of a ubiquitous, disruptive potential in European colonial ideologies of the nineteenth and twentieth centuries, an intertextual reading of the two narratives suggests that this potential can only be fully and effectively realized under specific material conditions. As Anne McClintock says,

> Seeking only the fissures of formal ambivalence (hybridity, ambiguity, undecidability and so on) cannot [. . .] explain the rise to dominance of certain groups or cultures, nor the dereliction and obliteration of others. To ask how power succeeds or fails—despite its provisionality and despite its constitution in contradiction and ambiguity—involves investigating not only the tensions of conceptual form but also the torsions of social history. (15)[13]

Read together with *Heart of Darkness, July's People* makes clear that limitations imposed by social and political conditions necessarily result in Marlow's and, to a lesser extent, Conrad's inability to break from the colonial discourse of their time—despite their intermittent sense of the contradictions and silences in that discourse. In this way, Gordimer's invocation of Conrad's novella helps to stress her point that white South Africans can only be prepared for a truly new national order if the material circumstances of their lives are transformed.

5

Struggling Toward the Postcolonial

The Ghost of Conrad in
Ama Ata Aidoo's *Our Sister Killjoy*

In "On National Culture," Franz Fanon rejects the notions of racial essence which he claims the native intellectual embraces—at one stage of development—in defensive reaction to the identities posited by colonial ideology:

> The unconditional affirmation of African culture has succeeded the unconditional affirmation of European culture. On the whole, the poets of negritude oppose the idea of an old Europe to a young Africa, tiresome reasoning to lyricism, oppressive logic to high-stepping nature, and on one side stiffness, ceremony, etiquette, and scepticism, while on the other frankness, liveliness, liberty, and—*why not?*—luxuriance. (213; italics mine)

Given the many Fanonian echoes within Ama Ata Aidoo's *Our Sister Killjoy*, as well as the narrator's rigorous debunking of essentialist racial ideology, it is no accident that Sissie, the novel's protagonist, uses the same expression as Fanon ("why not?") in her own experiments with the rhetoric of Negritude. Defensively seeking to counter the colonial discourse on race, Sissie thinks,

> No amount of pseudo-scientific junk is going to make us a weaker race than we are. [. . .] After all, what baby doesn't know that the glistening blackest coal also gives the hottest and the most sustained heat? Energy. Motion. We are all that. Yes, why not? (114–115)

Sissie again uses the expression "why not?" when she turns to the notion of a mystical and ideal African past in order to answer her boyfriend's claim that "the fact that [she and he] can meet and talk at all is an advantage to the present":

> In the old days, who knows, we could have been born in the same part of the land. Or we could have met when they brought me as a novice to understudy one of the famous priestesses in your area or when they sent you to be apprenticed to one of our goldsmiths. Maybe, it's all nostalgia and sentimental nonsense. Again, *why not?* Why should I be afraid of being sentimental? (115–116; italics mine)

Sissie acknowledges that an idealized conception of a precolonial African culture is probably another fairytale, although she does not recognize its dangers. Fanon claims such "sentimental nonsense" is "a blind alley" for the native intellectual because it leads away from the need to forge a national culture and towards the notion of a false cultural totality or unity on which the postcolonial future could be built (214).

Ironically, Aidoo's *Our Sister Killjoy* has repeatedly been read through a critical lens which relies on exactly the notion of a pre-existing, singular, postcolonial African identity that Fanon warned about. Kwaku Korang claims Aidoo "proposes the ethno-cultural imperative of knowing and affirming an African self [. . .] and the urgent task of recovering an Africanist mode of knowledge and being" (52). Similarly, Paula Morgan asserts that the text focuses on replacing "a white-eyed (Eurocentric) perspective with a black-eyed (Afrocentric) perspective" (193). And Elizabeth Willey writes that *Our Sister Killjoy* reevaluates "the intrusions of Islam and the West in Africa, in terms of an African view of history with the ultimate goal of establishing the African Personality" (15).

Concomitantly, as with the other African novels discussed in this study, when critics discuss the strong intertextual echoes of *Heart of Darkness* in *Our Sister Killjoy* they interpret these echoes as functioning primarily in order to challenge Conrad's "British," "colonial" perspective. According to C.L. Innes, in Aidoo's attempt to revise "the form and conventions of the novel as they have been handed down from British writers," she "rewrites and revises Conrad's *Heart of Darkness,* as the archetypal European novel about Africa" ("Mothers" 139–140). Innes goes on to claim

> Conrad's male European narrator, Marlowe [sic], recounting
> what he has learned from an earlier journey to the Congo, the
> heart of darkness, is challenged by Aidoo's female African narra-
> tor, Sissie, reflecting in the light of "knowledge gained since" on
> her youthful journey to Europe, and specifically to Bavaria, the
> heart of whiteness. (140)

Both homogenizing the Western literary tradition as a bearer of colonial
discourse and designating *Heart of Darkness* as the epitome of this tradition, Innes represents the intertextual relationship between it and *Our Sister Killjoy* as yet another instance of a postcolonial writing back, in which
fairly straightforward cultural binaries are preserved.[1]

Such a representation, however, ignores strong echoes in Aidoo's text
of Conrad's dialogic narrative form, which disrupts various kinds of
monologic discourses (such as those upon which the above critics seem to
rely). A primary component of Conrad's narrative structure is a scene of
storytelling in which the iconoclastic narrator Marlow offers a bildungsroman that not only describes the destabilizing of his younger self's
naive perspective but also disrupts his audience's smug cultural assumptions. The first narrator's simplistic colonial vision is made ridiculous by
Marlow's disturbing representations of his experiences in the Congo, even
as his desire for a narrative offering a clear and simple truth is mocked by
the ambiguity of "the horror" which offers the promise of, but refuses to
deliver, such a truth. The scene of storytelling also highlights Marlow's
belated effort to make sense of past events he did not understand at the
time; this aspect of his narration suggests the need to interrogate one's
own initial impressions of and explanations for past experience using—as
Aidoo puts it in *Our Sister Killjoy,* "knowledge gained since" (27). Even
more important, Conrad's novella includes a number of narrative devices
which dialogically bring into question the observations and representations Marlow offers as he tells his story. For example, Conrad encourages
the reader to interrogate Marlow's narration critically by putting it in quotation marks using the dual narration. Moreover, Marlow's own doubts
and uncertainty suggest he still has trouble understanding his experience
and that he questions many of his own conclusions. *Heart of Darkness*'s
form even forces the reader to engage in a dialogue with him- or herself.
Just as Marlow's tales frustrate the narrator, Conrad's novella defies readers' (especially students') expectations, created by the mixture of the quest
narrative and the bildungsroman form, of a final enlightenment offering
a dazzling truth. The ambiguity of "the horror" forces us to go back over

the entire narrative looking for clues to its meaning and frustrates the linear hermeneutic process. When confronted by skepticism towards Marlow's own construction of events encouraged by the narrative structure, readers can become more and more frustrated in their search for meaning as they are lead to doubt every conclusion they formulate.

The significance of *Heart of Darkness*'s dialogism is profound. It highlights the notion that all representations of the real are constructs, and it especially encourages a skepticism regarding both common hegemonic colonial representations and apparently oppositional perspectives. For example, if Marlow explicitly undermines Kurtz's narrative of a heroic imperialism both by revealing the absurdity of the notion of a spiritually transcendent European identity and by alluding to the horrors such a narrative generates, the narrative structure of *Heart of Darkness* also encourages the reader to examine how Marlow's own liberalism remains underpinned by the terms of colonial romance. Specifically, the narration encourages us to question Marlow's construction of a kind of European man who can keep his own savagery in check and so can possibly protect those (like the Africans) who cannot.

In ways quite similar to *Heart of Darkness, Our Sister Killjoy*'s narration also encourages a skepticism regarding various forms of colonial *and* anticolonial ideology, suggesting they often share discursive underpinnings and produce similar (colonial) effects. In this case, however, two separate characters—the narrator and Aidoo's protagonist Sissie—replace the single Marlow figure. Like Conrad, Aidoo has produced a bildungsroman in which the protagonist develops the ability to question hegemonic constructions of the real and a willingness to challenge such constructions in dialogue with others. At the same time, Aidoo's narrator serves similar functions to Marlow the storyteller not only by offering insightful commentary on Sissie's experience but also by emphasizing the gaps in Sissie's own initial understanding of her experiences and suggesting the need for narrative revision using the analytic tools accrued through maturation. Furthermore, Sissie's own reflections on her experiences in her concluding letter have many of the same stylistic qualities as Marlow's narration—they too ramble and turn back on themselves as Sissie tries to make sense of her experience and questions the explanations that she herself formulates. The letter also reveals that Sissie's process of maturation is not complete at the end of the narrative when she flies back to Ghana. To trace Sissie's education beyond this point, the reader must give up on the linear hermeneutic expectations created by the bildungsroman form and go back to earlier sections of the narrative in which the narrator indicates what Sissie will learn on her return to Africa.

Ultimately, however, *Our Sister Killjoy*—like *Heart of Darkness*—refuses to offer final answers to some important questions, and the resulting open-ended dialogism reinforces the distrust of monologic truths encouraged throughout the novel. In fact, Aidoo suggests the struggle against new forms of colonialism in a supposedly postcolonial world necessitates such a critical and skeptical perspective. Specifically, Aidoo indicates that a new, effective project of decolonization requires scepticism regarding the authoritative formulations of difference bequeathed by colonial and anticolonial rhetoric in the wake of national independence.[2] Echoing Frantz Fanon's arguments concerning national identity, *Our Sister Killjoy* insists that the development of a truly decolonized nation necessitates an open-ended, mobile approach to collective identity formation which resists a retreat to rigid, clear-cut binaries. As a result, Aidoo's novel repeatedly depicts "the blurring of roles":

> the distinctions between male and female, black and white, self and other, consumer and consumed, moral and immoral, are repeatedly constructed and deconstructed. The heroine's selves are multiple; there is no single authentic self to whom she can remain true by refusing the imposition of others. (Innes, "Conspicuous" 15)

This perspective on identity is tied to Aidoo's formal experimentation, in which, for example, she mixes poetry and prose in such a manner as to frustrate efforts to classify the text generically.

As I have suggested, in its encouragement of skepticism towards hegemonic and counterhegemonic ideologies, *Our Sister Killjoy* is similar to *Heart of Darkness,* and this affinity between the two texts makes it difficult to say the former simply reverses or writes back to the latter. Yet, it is also difficult to claim the texts have parallel perspectives. As Edward Said points out, *Heart of Darkness* may bring into question the terms of colonial ideology, but there is no possibility in Conrad's novella that the "dark places of the earth" could be governed by themselves rather than carved up as parts of European empires (*Culture* 30). In stark contrast, *Our Sister Killjoy* not only assumes the existence of an already differently organized world, but also focuses on the effort to construct identities that transform the concept of the nation inherited from European colonialism and nationalism. Just as importantly, Conrad's patriarchal vision in *Heart of Darkness* is utterly at odds with Aidoo's approach to gender and agency.

In *Our Sister Killjoy,* Sissie's progress towards maturation is measured through the enlightened perspective of the narrator. This perspective is characterized by rigorous political and historical reflection, resulting in an analysis both of the ways various subjectivities have been shaped by Western ideologies and institutions and of the functions these subjectivities serve. The narrator is especially concerned with how, as they are inhabited by the West's others, certain forms of subjectivity become a primary means by which Western exploitation of the non-Western world is perpetuated. For example, the narrator introduces Sissie's story with a scathing indictment of African elites who have been fully interpellated by their Western educations and who, as a result, blindly serve as agents for foreign interests. These elites regurgitate the language of universalism, "universal truth, universal art, universal literature, and the Gross National Product," which facilitates neocolonial exploitation both by masking the history of dispossession, a "reality that is more tangible than the massive walls of the slave forts standing along our beaches," and by creating a desire for European (i.e., universal) identity and all the trappings it entails (6). Because they have bought into a universalist rhetoric, they believe that their educations have bequeathed to them the authority of the West, but this belief only suppresses the reality of their roles as neocolonial puppets. Trying to take the position of the colonialist parental authority, suggesting "your problem is that you are too young" and "You must grow up," the African national bourgeoisie is in actuality "the dog of the house instead of the master" (6).

In the second section of *Our Sister Killjoy,* "The Plums," the narrator explores more fully the relationship between the elites and neocolonial exploitation. Describing Sissie's experience at the international German youth camp, the narrator explains she and others on scholarship do not think about why they are encouraged to gorge themselves: "They felt no need to worry over who should want them to be there eating. Why should they?" (35). By not reflecting on the control enabled by the desire for the European, the "campers" risk becoming cogs in a new colonial system which perpetuates unequal development: "Of course, later on when we have become / Diplomats / Visiting Professors / Local experts in sensitive areas / Or / Some such hustlers, / We would have lost even this small awareness, that in the first place, an invitation was sent [. . .]" (35).[3] This neocolonial dynamic takes its most deadly form in the structures of Africa's national governments. In the wake of independence, the new rulers' individual pursuit of the trappings of bourgeois European identity—including European wives—makes continued colonial exploitation even easier than it was under colonialism proper:

We have heard too, / Have we not / Of countries in / Africa where / Wives of Presidents hail from / Europe. / Bringing their brothers or [. . .] who knows? / To run the / Economy. / Excellent idea [. . .] / How can a / Nigger rule well / Unless his Balls and purse are / Clutched in / Expert White Hands [. . .] JUST LIKE THE GOOD OLD DAYS / BEFORE INDEPENDENCE / Except— / The present is / S-o-o-o much / Better! / For / In these glorious times when / Tubercular illiterates / Drag yams out of the earth with / Bleeding hands, / Champagne sippings Ministers and commissioners / Sign away / Mineral and timber / Concessions, in exchange for / Yellow wheat which / The people can't eat. / And at noon, / The wives drive Mercedes-Benzes to / Hairdressers', making ready for / The Evening's occasion / While on the market place, / The good yams rot for / Lack of transportation and / The few that move on, / Are shipped for Paltry cents— / To foreign places as / Pretty decorations / On luxury tables. (55–57)

The presidents and their cohorts are the contemporary Kurtzes of Africa; manipulated by their belief in a transcendence bequeathed by a European identity and their unrestrained desire for the goods of Europe, they are puppets of deadly and corrupt forces.

Yet, the narrator also suggests that African majorities contribute to their own impoverished and exploited condition because they too remain in the grip of the ideological equation between progress and the individual acquisition of European bourgeois identity. Specifically, these majorities remain blind to their betrayal by their leaders because they fail to disconnect the progress of the nation from their leaders' individual transcendence:

While / Able-bodied fishermen / Disappear in / Cholera, the rest, from under / Leaking roofs and unlit alleys / Shall drum, / and sing / dance with joy / This year of the pig-iron anniversary / Because / There is ecstasy / In dying from the hands of a / Brother / Who / Made / It. (58–59)

The narrator's perspective on the constructed subjectivities of the colonized and the purposes they serve necessitates a complex understanding of subject formation. *Our Sister Killjoy* suggests that, on the one hand, collective identities are social constructs and that, on the other, these constructs take on a certain materiality because of their relationship with power. The narrator outlines this perspective at the end of the first section when describing the moment Sissie becomes aware of race in the train station upon her arrival in Germany. When a woman says to her daughter, "Ja, das Schwartze Madchen," Sissie is confused ("Black girl? Black girl?") until she realizes there is a difference between her skin coloring and "the colour of the pickled pig parts" of "that crowd of people." Sissie's previous lack of awareness of race, despite her numerous interactions with Europeans, suggests that, rather than being a natural means of differentiating among people, it is a construct, and the fact that she is only made conscious of race when she arrives in Europe suggests it is a specifically European construct (12). The rejection of ideologies which attribute an essential moral or spiritual meaning to race is emphasized when the narrator tells us Sissie "was to regret this moment when she was made to notice differences in human colouring. No matter where she went, what anyone said, what they did. She knew it [human colouring] never mattered" (12–13).

However, the narrator also makes it clear that a rejection of racial thinking will need to be counterbalanced by an awareness of the way that constructed differences do matter because of their relationship with power (rather than because of their reflection of essential differences in moral, spiritual, and / or intellectual qualities):

> But what she also came to know was that someone somewhere would always see in any kind of difference, an excuse to be mean. / A way to get land, land, more land. / [. . .] A harsher edge to a voice. / A sharper ring to commands. / Power, Child, Power. / For this is all anything is about. / Power to decide / Who is to live, / who is to die. . . . (13)

This reflection on the political implications of difference, when combined with the seemingly contradictory claim that it "never mattered," suggests Sissie will need to balance two ways of approaching such difference. On the one hand, she will need to keep in mind that differential collective identities are always constructs. On the other hand, she must be aware of the ways such identities are given a certain reality because they are acted on and used as if they were real by those whose power is legitimated by them. The common link between these two understandings of difference is a recognition of the need to determine its significance in historical and political terms.

Our Sister Killjoy's critical stance towards ahistorical, essential conceptions of collective identity is also apparent when the narrator punctures the notion of a national spirit residing in the monuments of Germany by focusing on the historical realities suppressed by such a notion. The second section begins with a reference to a fairytale castle, "which the brochure tells you / Was one the largest in all / Germany," overlooking the river in the German town where Sissie stays, only to undermine the notion of a mythical past which it represents with an actual history of barbarism:

> So who was this / Prince [. . .] who had built one of / The largest castles of them all, / Possessed the / Biggest / Land, the / Greatest number of / Serfs? / How many / Virgins had / Our Sovereign Lord and Master / Unvirgined on their nuptial nights? (19)

Seen through a historical lens, the attraction of a quintessential German tourist monument turns into Marlow's "fascination of the abomination" (10). The narrator concludes the chapter with an even more specific attack on nationalist fairytales which equate place with a historically transcendent spirit of a people. Marija tells Sissie, "Munchen, Sissie, is our city, Bavaria. Our own city. [. . .] So beautiful you must see it, Sissie" (79). But the narrator claims,

> Marija, / There is nowhere in the / Western world that is a / Must- / No city is sacred, / No spot is holy. / Not Rome, / Not Paris, / Not London- / Nor Munich, Marija / And the whys and wherefores / Should be obvious. (79–80)

In Munich's case, these "whys and wherefores" include its relationships with the history of Nazi Germany: "Munich, Marija, / Is / The Original Adolf of the pub-brawls / and mobsters who were looking for / a / Fuhrer" (81). The narrator not only suggests that the meaning of the city cannot be separated from this history, but also points to the way that a German nationalist fairytale (Nationalist Socialism) resulted in the most obscene kind of horror. There is no guiding transcendent spirit in a place; as the narrator says, "Humans, / Not places, / Make memories" (81).

Heart of Darkness makes a similar point when it encourages the reader to question the first narrator's simplistic colonialist notion of Britain's "great spirit" that went out with its pirates and conquerors into the rest of the world (8). Marlow's story brings into question such an easy equation between identity, destiny, and place. Yet, at the same time, it cannot be denied that Aidoo's narrator's perspective is a corrective to the views of difference offered by Marlow, who constructs Africa as the embodiment of primordial darkness that determines the destiny of its people and represents Europe as having a long civilizational history, which has bequeathed to it institutions that enable the control of that darkness. (Thus, he says that in Europe "we" are used to looking at "the shackled form of a conquered monster," while "there" you can see it "monstrous and free" [37].) His questioning of an absolute biological or spiritual divide between Europe and Africa—as a result of the "ugly" kinship he "discovers" with Africans (38)—simply becomes a means to reconstitute nationalist identities in other terms. He may doubt the differential justification of colonial- . ism in much the same way as Aidoo's narrator, by claiming "the conquest of the earth, which mostly means the taking it away from those who have a different complexion or slightly flatter noses than ourselves, is not a pretty thing" (10), but he remains tied to the notions of identity on which imperialism is based—those excuses "to be mean." Similarly, *Heart of Darkness* itself may unravel the bases of Marlow's own analysis and narrative, but it remains ambivalent in its skewering of the terms of colonial discourse—for example, as Achebe has pointed out, by denying the Africans language. I would, however, argue that in its assault on nationalist identities, *Our Sister Killjoy* can be read as more fully attacking—writing back to—the rhetoric of Senghor's Negritude or Nkrumah's African Personality than to the kind of perspective offered by *Heart of Darkness*. The latter does encourage a skeptical approach to essentialist identities, even if it reinforces them; in contrast, Senghor and Nkrumah fully embrace notions of national spirit which *Our Sister Killjoy* suggests are dangerous fictions often used to support suspect interests.

In both *Our Sister Killjoy* and *Heart of Darkness,* the use of more knowledgeable narrators to trace the movement of initially naive protagonists from ignorance to knowledge is an important means by which dangerous hegemonic discourse is dialogically interrogated. (In the case of *Heart of Darkness,* the wiser story-teller—Marlow—actually narrates the development of a younger, more ignorant self.) At the beginning of *Our Sister Killjoy,* Sissie is very much like Marlow when he sets out on his journey into the Congo. Both are represented as having a sharpness of perception and a willingness to question that will eventually result in a narrowing of the gap between their own and the narrators' wiser perspectives. In this sense, both are different from the characters who surround them. Yet, both protagonists are depicted by the wiser narrators as initially having dangerous ideological naivete. For example, not yet questioning notions of European subjectivity, Marlow is initially unaware of the darkness within himself which will threaten to turn him into a Kurtz; similarly, believing in the benefits of Europe, Sissie does not recognize that her European scholarship is intended to groom her to become part of a (Kurtz-like) neocolonial elite. As *Heart of Darkness* and *Our Sister Killjoy* trace their respective protagonists' development, the contrast between their initial assumptions and what they come to know is an important means by which hegemonic perspectives are both evoked and undermined.

When we are first introduced to Sissie, she attends a dinner at the German ambassador's home after having just received her scholarship. This dinner "had been full of many things that puzzled her." For example, she does not understand why they went to such trouble: "Who did they think she was?" The clue is in the figure of the only other "African, a single man, her fellow countryman" (8). This man, who is called Sammy, is one of the elites indicted by the narrator. Like Kurtz, he serves colonial interests by mindlessly spouting the notion of an almost spiritual transcendence offered by Europe, even as his rhetoric masks his own degraded status. In this particular situation, repeating notions of European modernity is a potential means of producing more Sammies: "He was very anxious to get her to realize one big fact [. . .] that, somehow, going to Europe was altogether more like a dress rehearsal for a journey to paradise" (9). Sissie recognizes that something is wrong—she "shivered and fidgeted in her chair"—and she guesses that Sammy does serve a function: "Perhaps he had been invited to the dinner just to sing of the wonders of Europe?" (9). However, she does not know enough to understand the significance of Sammy's "singing." As the narrator already intimates, the desire for things European, including European identity, is the tool of colonial capitalism, which so completely inculcates this desire in the consciousness of the colonized, that the equation between Europe and progress is naturalized. Thus, of Sissie's departure, the narrator ironically comments, "Our Sister had made it" (9). Given the combination of the acerbic beginning of the book, the figure of Sammy, and the title of the first section ("Into a Bad Dream"), such a statement is read as double-voiced. The notion that, by going to Europe on a scholarship, one has "made it" might be a commonly accepted view among Sissie's fellow Ghanaians, but the narrator has given us plenty of reason to believe such scholarships usually result in their recipients becoming mindless puppets.

As the rest of the first section makes clear, developing the ability to question neocolonial discourse is extremely difficult because of its relationship with the material operation of colonial capitalism. For example, in the description of Sissie's walk among the shops of a train station when she first arrives in Germany, the narrator suggests how the distribution of consumer goods creates desire for the European and reinforces the notion of Europe's centrality. Sissie is entranced by the quality and quantity of the merchandise, "Feasting her village eyes" on "polished steel. Polished tin. Polished brass. Cut glass. Plastic." (12). Yet, her greedy visual consumption is not the result of premodern consciousness coming in contact with the modern but stems from a global order imposed by European capitalism; as Sissie herself observes, "this must be where those 'Consumer Goods' trickled from, to delight so much the hearts of the folks at home. Except here, they were not only a million times more, but also a thousand times better" (12).

In terms of Sissie's development, this scene works in two ways. First, we observe the beginning of her education as she becomes aware of how European capitalism assigns differential material positions to Ghana and Germany. Second, she is too overwhelmed to follow through with the implications of her observations. The hyperbole ("a million times more" / "a thousand times better") serves to emphasize the degree to which her consumption—the "feasting" of her eyes—hampers her critical facility; at this point, the differential operation of capitalism successfully prevents her from interrogating the desire it generates. In this sense, the scene echoes *Heart of Darkness,* focusing both on the need to resist a powerful force which attracts, controls, and, ultimately, degrades (what Marlow calls "the fascination of the abomination") and on the difficulty of achieving such resistance because of the power of the attraction.

In the second section, Europe's dangerous attractions for its others is embodied in the eponymous plums. Sissie has only had access to this fruit in inferior form in Ghana; she "had never seen plums before she came to Germany. No, she had never seen real, living, plums. Stewed prunes, yes. Dried, stewed, sugared-up canned plums [. . .] learning to take / Desserts—true mark of a leisured class— / Canned prunes / Canned pears / Canned apples" (38–39). As when Sissie was confronted with the superior manufactured goods in the train station, when she sees fresh plums, the combination of her previous experience and the luster of these plums results in unthinking rapture and consumption: "It was midsummer and the fruit stalls were overflowing. She had decided that being fruits, she liked them all, although her two loves were going to be pears and plums. And on those two she gorged herself" (39).

The danger of Sissie's desire is reflected in her relationship with Marija, the German woman who uses, among other foods, her plums as a means of seduction: "They were of a size, sheen, and succulence she had not encountered anywhere else in those foreign lands" (40). Initially, Sissie greedily consumes Marija's plums, because of their wondrous qualities and of "other qualities that [Sissie] herself possessed at that material time: / Youthfulness / Peace of mind / Feeling free: / Knowing you are a rare article, / Being / Loved." Young and naive, Sissie is unaware that she is being positioned as a "rare article" to be consumed by Marija.

However, when Marija actually makes a pass at her, Sissie has a revelation concerning the hidden horrors linked with the desire for and consumption of Europe's bounty. (The problem with this attempted seduction is not that it involves two women. In fact, the narrator suggests that the moral proscription of homosexuality—calling it "a / c-r-i-m-e / A sin / S-o-d-o-m-y"—is the result of prudish Victorian values. Instead, Aidoo condemns the predatory aspect of Marija's actions and the sexual exoticizing of Sissie.) Having been coaxed by Marija upstairs into the bedroom, Sissie becomes aware of the woman's hands on her body: "As one does from a bad dream, impulsively, Sissie shook herself free" (64). When connected with the title of the first chapter, "Into a Bad Dream," the narrator's statement suggests this moment represents a liberation from the ideology of European modernity. This is reinforced by Sissie's rush of thoughts in which a childhood memory of being with her mother—the memory of a nonexploitative relationship and a safe place—is contrasted with questions about her current home:

And now where was she? How did she get there? What strings, pulled by whom, drew her into those pinelands where not so long ago human beings stoked their own funeral pyres with other human beings, where now a young aryan housewife kisses a young black woman with such desperation, right in the middle of her own nuptial chamber, with its lower middle-class cosiness? A love-nest in an attic that seems to be only a nest now, with love gone into mortgage and holiday hopes? (64)

Sissie's questions reflect an interrogation of the fairytale of Europe. Asking what Europe is and what underlying causes have brought her there, she now thinks of it in terms of past and present horrors and distrusts its intentions. She recognizes that Marija's loneliness and need are the result of the forms of subjectivity which capitalism itself spawns and which drive Marija and her husband to consume excessively even though the result is that he must constantly work. The couple's subsequent alienation from

each other, and its causes, are embodied in those beauty products in the
bedroom on which they have spent money but which remain unneeded:
"They all looked expensive. Yet with a number of them also still in their
packaging, nothing looked over-used" (63).

Although this scene represents an important development for Sissie,
her perspective should not necessarily be equated with the position of the
text—especially at such an early moment in the narration. Throughout
the first three sections of *Our Sister Killjoy*, the narrator points to the
problems with Sissie's conclusions and to the gaps in her knowledge, thus
suggesting a continued need for maturation. In fact, at this point in the
narrative, Aidoo uses one of Sissie's epiphanies to evoke rhetoric that simply reverses the terms of colonial ideology and that the text as a whole
brings into question. Seeing Marija begin to cry, Sissie envisions her loneliness as an allegory for Europe: "Suddenly Sissie knew. She saw it once
and was never to forget it. She saw against the background of the thick
smoke that was like a rain cloud over the chimneys of Europe, / LONE-
LINESS / Forever falling like a tear out of a woman's eye" (65). Sissie
thinks of Europeans' "loneliness" as the cause for their drive to master
lands and peoples deemed other. In other words, Sissie constructs a hollowness at the heart of Europe, which it tries to fill through colonialism:

> And so this was it? / Bullying slavers and slave-traders. / Solitary
> discoverers. / Swamp-crossers and lion hunters. / Missionaries
> who risked the cannibal's pot to / bring the world to the heathen
> hordes. / Speculators in gold in diamond uranium and / copper /
> [. . .] Miserable rascals and wretched whores whose only dis-
> tinction in life was that at least they were better than the
> Natives. (65–66)

If one assumes Sissie's perspective represents the perspective of the text
itself, then this moment is evidence that *Our Sister Killjoy* reverses *Heart
of Darkness*. Marlow suggests that in Africa he finds the heart of a primordial darkness unrestrained by European civilization. In stark contrast,
Sissie's travel in Europe have revealed to her a corrosive heart of whiteness
which has its origins in European civilization and which spreads misery
throughout the world; this civilization becomes Sissie's horror. Yet, given
the complex perspective on identity offered by *Our Sister Killjoy*, Sissie's
characterization of the colonizer, while it certainly represents a kind of
insight, remains seriously flawed. At this moment, she homogenizes the
European other by turning Marija into an allegory of all Europeans, and

she creates an overly easy distinction between that other and the self by locating the sole cause of the colonial drive in a quality in "them" and in "their" place.

The relationship between Marija and Sissie actually reflects the problems with Sissie's conception of the link between identity and place. Stuck in traditional gender roles (mother / housewife), Marija seeks some kind of fulfillment in the exotic by pursuing Sissie. In this pursuit, she takes on the role of the male seducer—especially in the scene in the bedroom. Yet, at the same time, she has placed herself in a subservient female role by cooking for and waiting on Sissie. More generally, Marija's confinement and Sissie's relative freedom and agency complicate the relations of power and vulnerability in the relationship. In other words, the impact of gender on this relationship and the ambiguities it creates subtly disrupts rigid representations of identity based on geographical or racial dichotomies.

The disruptive significance of gender for Sissie's epiphany is made especially clear when Sissie tells Marija of her imminent departure and finds that she takes pleasure in her exercise of emotional power:

> Clearly, she was enjoying herself to see that woman hurt. It was nothing she had desired. Nor did it seem as if she could control it, this inhuman sweet sensation to see another human being squirming. It hit her like a stone, the knowledge that there is pleasure in hurting. A strong three-dimensional pleasure, an exclusive masculine delight that is exhilarating beyond all measure. (76)

The phrase, "an exclusive masculine delight," points to the way gender is a significant form of difference used to define identity and distribute power. Yet, the irony of Sissie's experiencing this "delight" undermines the kind of essentializing collective binaries entailed by the modifiers "exclusive masculine" and suggests the limitations of an understanding of identity based on such binaries. Sissie's feelings also directly undermine the equation she drew earlier between geographical identity and the desire for the power a colonial system affords. She had suggested these feelings among Europeans were the result of a loneliness that was particular to them, but at this moment, Sissie too gets a pleasurable feeling from the exercise of a similar kind of power over another.

The importance of Sissie's persistant limitations regarding an understanding of identity and identity formation are made manifest in the narrator's discussion of her reactions when she first arrives in England. Not yet grasping how the subjectivity of the formerly colonized is called into being by colonial ideology and how such interpellation leads them to actively participate in their own continued subjection, Sissie does not understand why there is a large population of miserable black immigrants from the ex-colonies who do the most degrading forms of menial labor and who all claim to be students. The narrator explains these students come because they are enticed by the notion that England and, especially, a British education are the means to progress:

> the story is as old as empires. Oppressed multitudes from the provinces rush to the imperial seat because that is where they know all salvation comes from. But as other imperial subjects in other times and places have discovered, for the slave, there is nothing at the centre but worse slavery. (87–88)

Although she is infuriated by this "slavery," Sissie remains unable to engage in the kind of causal analysis offered by the narrator:

> Our poor sister. So fresh. So touchingly naive then. She was to come to understand that such migrations are part of the general illusion of how well an unfree population think they do for themselves. Running very fast just to remain where they are. She wondered why they never told the truth of their travels at home. Not knowing that if they were to keep on being something in their own eyes, then they could not tell the truth to their own selves or to anyone else. (89)

The narrator emphasizes Sissie's ignorance of the self-perpetuating dynamics of neocolonial exploitation. These immigrants' very conception of themselves is based on the status bequeathed by the notion of a transcendence acquired in Europe. Because this notion underpins their sense of self-worth, the immigrants encourage it both passively, by not telling the "truth of their travels," and actively, by emphasizing their supposed privileged status when they return: "They lied. / The Been-tos lied. / And another generation got itself ready to rush out" (90).

Although the third section emphasizes Sissie's continued need for maturation, it also reveals she has developed what the narrator refers to as a "black-eyed squint" (93)—a way of looking at the world that brings into question reductive and politically suspect perspectives using historically informed analysis. Just as important, she begins to display a willingness to challenge these perspectives in dialogue—a willingness not displayed during her stay in Germany, even when she begins to cultivate a skeptical vision. As claimed earlier, throughout *Our Sister Killjoy* the narrator suggests that change necessitates more than just the private analysis of monologic notions of the real; one must actively challenge such notions in dialogue with others. For example, there is the need to confront publicly the vision of Europe encouraged by the been-tos if "another generation" is to be discouraged from rushing "out." In the last two sections, as Sissie engages in combative dialogue, she makes others upset and angry because she is offering a perspective that challenges ways of envisioning the world with which they are comfortable. As the narrator says, it is "quite obvious that the world is not filled with folks who shared our sister's black-eyed squint at things" (93). Consequently, when Sissie shares her squint in dialogue (the subtitle of the book is *Reflections of a black-eyed squint*), she becomes "sister killjoy." Sissie has become very much like the more mature Marlow, who tries to disrupt the unquestioned assumptions of his listeners and, consequently, makes them defensive. (The smug first narrator in *Heart of Darkness* ridicules Marlow's stories because they unsettle his simple and certain understanding of the real.)

In an interaction with a Scottish woman, Sissie challenges easy formulations of oppressed identity which mask the actual relationships determined by contemporary imperial history. The woman tells Sissie, "we have a lot in common" because "we had chiefs like you who fought and all, while the Invader marched in" (91). Sissie "felt that their kinship had better end right there" and responds by pointing out the participation of the Scottish in the colonization of Africa. She reminds the woman of "Livingstone the Saint" and the "Scottish missions everywhere / In Tumu-Tumu and Mampong" (92). When the woman "screamed" that Sissie should not judge "Scotland / By her traitors," Sissie "politely" tells her that "She couldn't really judge, / Seeing / Her cute degree in English Hons., / Was gotten / From Burns / Bruce / and / McPherson" (92). Sissie reminds the woman of the culpability of the Scottish not only because of their direct participation in the establishment of the British empire, but also because of their contribution to cultural tools which helped maintain it. Repeatedly in the third section we see this contrast between Sissie's historicizing perspective and the ahistorical and reductive perspectives of those with whom she interacts, as well as her desire to challenge these suspect perspectives in combative dialogue.

A particularly dangerous perspective is offered by Kunle who joyously celebrates the transplant of a young black man's heart into the chest of an old white man in South Africa by a white South African surgeon. Kunle offers a universalist vision of the transplant's significance, claiming it represents an important step towards the eradication of racism since it reveals a common humanity: "he was sure it is the / type of development that can / solve the question of apartheid / and rid us, African negroes / and all other negroes of the / Colour Problem" (96). Sissie, in contrast, understands the situation in socioeconomic terms, seeing it as a form of continued exploitation that is enabled by colonial racism:

> Sissie had wanted to tell Kunle that our hearts and other parts are more suitable (than animals) for surgical experiments in aid of the Man's health and longevity. Because although we are further from human beings than dogs or cats, by some dictate of the ever-capricious Mother nature, our innards are more like the Man's than dogs or cats? (100)

However, although Sissie wants "to tell" and apparently even tries, Kunle will not listen: "Kunle was obviously in touch with reasonable well-informed circles. And just an attempt on Sissie's part to open her mouth to contradict anything he had to say got him mad" (101). Kunle is one of the neocolonial elites condemned by the narrator; programmed by his education, he spouts a language of universalism, which masks real political and economic relations, and refuses to listen to alternative perspectives because he believes his European education has given him an intellectual transcendence.

However, although Sissie's interactions with those like the Scottish woman and Kunle clearly reveal her maturation, even in these interactions the narrator continues to allude to the incomplete nature of her education. For example, in introducing the dialogue with the Scottish woman, the narrator suggests her assertion of kinship could be read as accurate. This claim attunes the reader to the limitations of Sissie's own perspective and to what she herself could learn from the dialogue. Because the Scots who participated in empire building were among the "day-and-night watchmen of the Empire" and not "the real owners," they served the same function as the African neocolonial elites do in the present: "There must be a Mensah in every town, / Every region its Sambo" (91). As a result, "The grey Menopausing Lady-on-the-bus" did "make sense after all"; there are important ways commonality can be established among the many groups conquered by the British. Recognizing this connection can help establish a better understanding of the operations of empire and its long-term effects. The Scottish woman makes an important point when she observes Britain has enriched and empowered itself using the labor and skill of its Scottish subjects without them even being aware of the ways they were contributing to their own colonized condition: "Ach, what waste our men and brains! / What could / England have done without / Scottish shipping too? Fleming / Discovering / Penicillin / For England / to / Glory in?" (92).

In the description of the interaction with Kunle, the narrator suggests that, despite Sissie's insightful opposition to his perspective on the transplant, she remains to some degree entrapped by the notions of a European education to which he subscribes. When he first expresses his view of the transplant, Sissie does not express her thoughts fully, admonishing "herself to tread / Softly—We are in the region of / SCIENCE! / Little / Village / Girls / who / Dream / Do not / Cannot / Ever / Understand / These things" (96). In the final section, "Love Letter," Sissie's further maturation will be revealed by her ability and willingness to challenge persistently and publicly the kind of views offered by Kunle, even when they are articulated by the most educated of her countrymen.

The importance of mounting such a challenge is emphasized at the end of the third section when the narrator explains the circumstances of Kunle's death. Kunle returns to Ghana to help his family and his nation, but he returns as the been-to hero who assumes the role of the colonizer as a result of his education: "life 'home' had its compensations. The aura of having been overseas at all. Belonging to the elite, whatever that is" (107). Trying to uphold his elite image, Kunle not only buys a car but also hires a chauffeur: "what is the point in owning a special car in Africa if you are going to drive yourself to your village?" (107). The result is a deadly car accident which, both in its causes and effects, is an example of the neocolonial condition. Not only has his colonialist conception of identity led him to buy a (European) car and hire a chauffeur, it has also resulted in his taking out a European insurance policy which does not pay off:

> for although the policy had been absolutely comprehensive, the insurance people had insisted it did not cover a chauffeur driving at 80 m.p.h. on the high road. [. . .] And like all of us who have been to foreign places, Kunle could recognize quality service when he saw it. He had taken out his policy with a very reliable insurance company [. . .] Foreign, British, terribly old and solid.

This conclusion of Kunle's story emphasizes how the heart transplant represents colonial dispossession in which the hearts of Europe's others—

their labor, resources, professionals, and very lives—are used to give new life to Europe. In contrast with Conrad's vague heart imagery, which (like "the horror") is so abstract as to embody the impossibility of ever arriving at a conclusive meaning, the heart in *Our Sister Killjoy* has a material and historical significance that serves to undermine the kind of universalizing abstractions embraced by Kunle and encouraged by *Heart of Darkness.*

The final section, comprised primarily of the letter Sissie writes to her boyfriend on the flight back to Ghana, represents her own efforts to under-stand the means by which the present is colonized and to find a way out of the neocolonial condition. In the letter, Sissie recounts and continues a series of debates with her boyfriend and other educated exiles like Kunle in which she focuses on the perpetuation of colonial dynamics in a supposedly postcolonial world and undermines the exiles' smug embrace of European modernity. However, the letter reflects how she struggles with many of her own conclusions which threaten to elide the complexity of the path to decolonization. In fact, this letter generates more questions than answers. It reveals to the reader that although Sissie's return to Africa represents a nec-essary step in her effort to find the postcolonial, it is not equated with lib-eration. The letter also establishes the clearest connections between *Our Sis-ter Killjoy* and *Heart of Darkness* in terms of form. Marlow's narration consistently brings into question his own perspective as he enacts a kind of debate with himself and acknowledges the excess that perspective fails to account for. This aspect of Marlow's narration, perhaps more than any other element of the novella's form, encourages a profound skepticism towards his narrative and resists closure to *Heart of Darkness*'s dialogism.

At the beginning of her letter, Sissie uses memories of her debates with her boyfriend about the use of English and its significance as a springboard to articulate the need for a postcolonial language and culture and to explore the means by which they might be created. She recalls that when he tried to counter her "negativism" concerning their use of Eng-lish, she claimed her reliance on the colonial language represented a con-tinued colonization of her "self":

> Eh, My Love, what positive is there to be, when I cannot give voice to my soul and still have her heard? Since so far, I have only been able to use a language that enslaved me, and therefore, the messengers of my mind always come shackled? (112)

Sissie acknowledges the potential accuracy of her boyfriend's response that the use of English does not necessarily result in mental colonization, but

she insists that they both remain psychically colonized and that the continued use of colonial languages reflects this condition. The comment
about being "enslaved" by English is to be understood "symbolically,
referring to the many areas of our lives where we are unable to operate
meaningfully because of what we have gone through" (113). Sissie points
to the need to understand the psychic and cultural impact of the colonial
past in order to escape a colonized present and move towards a postcolonial future. She acknowledges her boyfriend is right when he insists the
way to the future is to let "time move," but she rejects his claim that this
can happen by ignoring history. Such an assertion elides the need to
understand the paths laid out by colonialism in order to find ways of
operating "meaningfully" which will "give [time] something to carry [. . .]
something we value" (113).

As Sissie moves further into her letter, she still struggles to find the
path out of her colonized ("shackled") condition and towards a postcolonial culture and identity. To some degree, Sissie acknowledges that a postcolonial culture is something to be created rather than simply reclaimed:

> In any case, the question is not just the past or the present, but
> which factors out of both the past and the present represent for
> us the most dynamic forces for the future. That is why, above
> all, we have to have our secret language. We must create this
> language. It is high time we did. We are too old a people not
> to. (116)

As a number of critics note, Sissie's recognition of the need to create a
postcolonial language corresponds with Aidoo's own efforts to explode the
conventions of written English in the form of *Our Sister Killjoy*, and
Sissie's claim of the need to choose from past and present corresponds
with Aidoo's use of both oral and written literary forms.[4] In this sense,
Sissie's recipe for a postcolonial culture corresponds with the perspective
of the text.

Once again, however, the text's perspective should not be equated too
closely with Sissie's. When she says "we are too old a people not to" create a new postcolonial language, she suggests a decolonized culture will be
grounded in the interests of an African collective (the "us" in the preceding passage), which is defined by an already existing precolonial identity.
In this sense, Sissie echoes Nkrumah's notion of an "African Personality"
which reflects a singular precolonial African consciousness and which
forms the basis for the postcolonial nation:

There is a searching after Africa's regeneration—politically, socially and economically—within the milieu of a social system suited to the traditions, history, environment and communal pattern of African society. Notwithstanding the inroads made by western influences, this still remains unchanged. In the vast rural areas of Africa, the people still hold land in common and work on it in cooperation. These are the main features still predominating in African society and we cannot do better than to bend them to the requirements of a more modern socialistic pattern of society. (Nkrumah 162–163)

Our Sister Killjoy problemetizes this notion of an already existing African collective which would define itself in terms of a common set of interests. For example, the narrator points to the horrors of a stratified society in precolonial African history by comparing "the Abome kings of Dahomey" with "The Third Reich" (36–37). The narrator also repeatedly refers to the divisions in both past and present created by gender. Commenting on Marija's happiness that her only child was a boy, the narrator claims that any

> good woman / In her senses / [. . .] Would say the / Same / [. . .] Anywhere: / For / Here under the sun, / Being a woman / Has not / Is not / Cannot / Never will be a / Child's game / From knowledge gained since— / So why wish a curse on your child / Desiring her to be female / ? / Besides, my sister, / The ranks of the wretched are / Full, / Are full. (51)

Finally, as the narrator's descriptions of the neocolonial condition have made clear, the African present remains colonized, not only materially but also psychically. When she goes back to Africa, Sissie is not returning to a unified and valorized African communal consciousness on which a postcolonial Ghana can be based, as most critics have suggested;[5] this consciousness, like the culture to which it will be inextricably tied, must be forged, in part by making people aware of their common interests (resulting from colonial and neocolonial history) and in part by combating those factors which create competing sets of identities and interests.

Despite problems with Sissie's formulation of the path to decolonization, *Our Sister Killjoy* suggests she is moving in the right direction through her struggles with others and herself and through her decision to return to Africa. Again and again, the narrator suggests decolonization necessitates the reversal of the dispossession of the African majorities by the West. If Sissie is to contribute to such a reversal, she must return to Ghana to work with the dispossessed using her "black-eyed squint" and undermine the ideologies of colonialism and modernity which are so crucial for the operation of neocolonialism. In contrast, remaining in Europe, even with her black-eyed squint, would contribute to the flow of human resources out of Africa and to the perpetuation of notions of modernity—of the equation between Europe and progress—which keep this flow going. Only by a material as well as discursive rejection of the roles and directions offered her by the neocolonial global system can she work against that system.

That Sissie's return to Ghana is based on an understanding of these factors is revealed by her record of her debates with the African educated exiles. Sissie is disturbed by the continued drain of resources from Africa represented by these exiles, not only because of the loss of much-needed skills but also because those skills have been developed at the direct expense of the impoverished majority. As she points out to one group of exiles, they are part of the "thousands all over the western world who were brought here and maintained by government scholarships, and who have refused, consistently, to go back home after graduation" (126). At the same time, these educated elites reinforce hegemonic notions of progress that fuel dispossession by measuring success using the standards of a European bourgeois modernity. For example, the young surgeon, who represents Sissie's most formidable interlocutor, claims to be tackling colonial racism by proving to Europeans that an African can be as accomplished as the best European in terms of aquiring formal education, wealth, and professional fame: "you can see how by remaining here someone like me serves a very useful purpose in educating them to recognize our worth" (129). In response, Sissie points to the material dispossession which his remaining in Europe represents, alludes to the dangers of his acceptance of the principles of colonial modernity, and appeals to him to reverse the neocolonial process:

> if we are not careful, we would burn out our brawn and brains trying to prove what you describe as "our worth" and we won't get a flicker of recognition from those cold blue eyes. And anyway, who are they? [. . .] So please come home. (130)

Sissie eventually sees the futility in appealing to the educated immigrants like the young doctor (the Sammies) who will not let go of the system upon which their egos and individual privilege are based. On the plane, she decides not to send the letter to her boyfriend—who she knows is like the doctor—since it will not "do much good" (133). She recognizes she must return to Africa to continue her struggle against neocolonialism and forge a path to a postcolonial future.

The novel ends when Sissie, having just finished her letter on the flight, decides "she didn't care" if the "occupant of the next seat probably thought she was crazy" because "she had spoken aloud to herself" (133–134); this lack of concern with the codes of conventional behavior reflects a general willingness to transgress the dictates of hegemonic reason or Gramscian common sense. In stark contrast with Kunle, Sissie goes back with her "crazy" black-eyed squint—the unexpected resource she has acquired from her stay in Europe—which gives her an understanding of how specific Western ideologies bequeath identities and directions to its others that enable unequal global development. As a result, she has the potential to help those most fully dispossessed by this process through contributing to the interrogation and understanding of the underlying means—both psychic and material—which enable their dispossession.

Yet, Sissie is not represented as a been-to heroine going back to Ghana with knowledge that will enable her to lead "the people" out of their colonial darkness and into the bright postcolonial future. Such a symbolic figure would reinscribe the dangerous notion that salvation emanates from Europe (and especially from a European education) and minimize the difficulty of transcending the colonial present and formulating a postcolonial future. (In similar fashion, in *Heart of Darkness,* if Marlow were able to offer an unproblematic "idea" that would redeem colonialism, the focus on a ubiquitous darkness, which corrupts even the most apparently noble of colonial endeavors, would be attenuated.) Instead, the narrator repeatedly alludes to ways Sissie's education will continue and to revisions her perspective will undergo once she returns to Africa. Just as important, her own letter reveals she returns to Ghana still struggling to formulate a viable form of agency which can ground the struggle against neocolonialism.

As a result of its focus on the transformative potential in dialogue, *Our Sister Killjoy* suggests that Sissie's continuing education and development will result from her interactions with others in Ghana who will offer her perspectives which will complicate her own vision of the real—including her envisioning of communal identity. In Fanonian terms, Sissie goes back to shake *and* be shaken by the people; in these dialogic interactions she will become aware that the identity of the people is being constructed, and that, with her black-eyed squint, she is part of this unstable and open-ended process. She is one of the intellectuals who, according to Fanon:

> must join [the people] in that fluctuating movement which they are just giving a shape to, and which, as soon as it has started, will be the signal for everything to be called in question. Let there be no mistake about it; it is to this zone of occult instability where the people dwell that we must come. (227)

Although the fact and manner of Sissie's return represents a rejection of the roles and directions offered her by hegemony, she goes back neither having uncovered an existing postcolonial identity nor embodying a new one (there are no such dazzling conclusions here), but already in the "zone of occult instability" which, in its fluctuation and uncertainty, represents the path to the postcolonial. This liminality is reflected in the final scene which leaves Sissie suspended in air between Europe and Africa and emphasizes transition rather than arrival.

In *Our Sister Killjoy,* the instability of identity has an important temporal dimension. Aidoo suggests that the struggle against neocolonialism necessitates a narrative act of return and rereading in which the past is revisited in the light of the present (and vice versa). This process disrupts the established meanings of both past and present and produces new knowledge. For example, the narrator emphasizes not only what Sissie learned through her experiences in Europe but also what is to be learned from narrating her travels using the knowledge she has gained since her return. This emphasis, on the need to return to and reread the past in order to move into the future, is also built into the hermeneutic process of the reader, who, upon finishing the text, is encouraged to revisit the rest of the narrative in order to trace Sissie's continued development after she returns to Ghana. This is one of the ways *Our Sister Killjoy* departs from and exploits the generic expectations of the bildungsroman. Like *Heart of Darkness,* it appears to offer a story of development, in which the protagonist moves linearly towards an understanding of herself, her world, and her place in it. Yet, just as the reader must look back at Marlow's reflections on his experiences throughout his narrative in order to try to figure out what "the horror" might mean, the reader of Aidoo's novel must—after moving through the narrative linearly—look back at the narrator's commentary in the first three sections in order both to follow Sissie's temporal development as far as the narrative will allow, and to try to answer the important questions posed by her letter—especially the question of who the "we" is that represents the grounding for a postcolonial identity and culture.

Ultimately, however, both texts frustrate the search for final, unambiguous answers to some of the key questions they pose. Just as *Heart of Darkness* refuses to divulge the meaning of "the horror," *Our Sister Killjoy* does not offer a clear, unambiguous collective identity on which to base the postcolonial. The closest we come is the identity and perspective of the narrator. This narrator is inextricably connected with, and perhaps even embodies, a sense of collective identity (the narrator is never signified in individual terms) in relation to which Sissie herself will be able to define a productive, postcolonial conception of agency. This collective identity represents a movement away from a bourgeois focus on the individual and individual interests and, more generally, a resistance against the most deep-seated ideological effects of colonialism. Yet, in accordance with the text's emphasis on the historically contingent and fluid nature of collective identity and on the questionable political purposes to which static, secure representations of it are put, part of the enlightenment represented by the narrator includes a warning against closing off the process of identity formation. For example, the collectivity with which the narrator is associated, designated by the "our" of the title, remains ambiguous. At times, the "we" includes and even refers to the educated elites, at others it designates the impoverished African majorities; it can be gendered but often is not; it can even encompass a general humanity. This ambiguity of identity extends to the generic classification of the text itself, which crosses between poetry and prose in a manner that makes it impossible to characterize. Such ambiguity has three important implications: it encourages an interrogation of static, singular conceptions of identity which many forms of anticolonial nationalism embrace; it focuses attention on the need *to create* a not yet existing collective identity (rather than uncovering an already existing one) that will become a basis for resistance against the operation of colonial capitalism; and it suggests this creative process must remain fluid, ever open to revision—much like the process of Sissie's education itself.

As I have suggested, in its lack of closure, *Our Sister Killjoy* is very similar to *Heart of Darkness*. Both texts encourage skepticism, not only towards more overt forms of hegemonic discourse, but also towards seemingly alternative means of representation. More generally, both texts disrupt the formulation of stable, monologic truths. Yet, there are some important disjunctions resulting from the kind of contingent historical differences which Aidoo's narrator repeatedly suggests cannot be ignored. One of these disjunctions is epitomized, ironically, by the central ambiguities in the two texts. In *Heart of Darkness,* that ambiguity is the "horror" which both encourages a focus on a timeless human condition and pessimistically suggests there is little hope for a better world. In contrast, the central ambiguity in *Our Sister Killjoy* is the postcolonial "we," which must be defined in terms of specific historical and political conditions and which, especially in conjunction with Sissie's development, invokes a certain optimism. These differences would be supported by *Heart of Darkness'* undermining of all grounding for collective identity and action. Conrad's novella offers a single narrator who necessarily remains separated from his listeners as a result of the supposedly individualistic nature of subjectivity and the impossibility of knowing another. In stark contrast, Aidoo offers us a narrator who is never individuated from a collective "we" and who does know and understand the protagonist and her experience.

Another striking difference between *Heart of Darkness* and *Our Sister Killjoy* is in the representation of women. Conrad's women remain, as Marlow says, "out of it—completely" (49)—i.e., "out of touch with truth" (16). They are unable to live and act in the real world and so "stay in that beautiful world of their own" (49). As a result, women (like the Intended) are reliant on men (like Marlow) to protect them from reality. There are no representations of women in *Heart of Darkness* which contradict this characterization, and Marlow himself expresses no doubt about his judgment on the matter. In contrast, Aidoo offers us a female protagonist who is the one character able to gain real insight and, as a result, act effectively. Not only is she unafraid to challenge the myths embraced by the male exiles, but she refuses to follow the path laid out for her by traditional gender roles when she neither appeases nor follows "her man." As she says in her letter,

> all sorts of well-wishers have told me what I should have done in the first place, loving you as much as I claim to. [. . .] They say that any female in my position would have thrown away everything to be with you: first her opinions, and then her own plans. [. . .] What did I rather do but daily and loudly criticize you and your friends for wanting to stay forever in alien places. (117)

Yet in its representation of gender, *Our Sister Killjoy* can be read as writing back as much to a certain trend in African literature as to literary texts by male European writers like Conrad. Kwaku Korang claims Aidoo undermines the passive, disempowering images of women projected by African male writing and attacked so forcefully by Florence Stratton in her study of the "mother Africa trope": "Where representations of the African woman in Africanist literary discourse have consigned her to an ontological location that belied her agency, it it characteristic of Aidoo's vigorous language to make woman's voice *heard*" (53).[6] In other words, even on the issue of gender *Our Sister Killjoy*'s intertextual relationships reinforce the need for a critical dialogue with numerous overlapping ideologies representing a complex configuration of subject positions. Only such a dialogue, which escapes the bonds of rigid binaries, will lead the way to true national liberation.

CONCLUSION

The Question of Political Agency

I conclude by offering some brief comments on the implications of this study for questions of political agency. The foregoing literary readings break from the kind of postcolonial theoretical approach—perhaps most closely associated with Homi Bhabha—which assumes the primacy of the textual (over the material) and valorizes the deconstructive at the expense of the referential. In focusing on the dismantling of all grounding for collective identities and agents, this approach leaves us (as many critics note) with a bourgeois politics of the individual subject (understood as a constructive absence). In contrast, the readings in this study have explored how the African fiction I have examined is concerned with material *and* discursive conditions of oppression and exploitation and with the concomitant need for a conception of communal identity which will effectively contribute to the struggle for liberation, especially in the face of arrested decolonization. In none of these novels is the individual free from material determinates to shape the self using a deconstructive and ironic vision; that is, in none of them can difference/absence alone be a sign of power and freedom.

Yet, these novels also emphasize the difficulty of trying to understand and represent forms of agency on which nonoppressive political mobilization could be based. There is often an awareness of the ways the categories used in the past suppressed internal divisions and enabled new forms of colonialism and ongoing imperial exploitation. Such awareness can be linked with a more general skepticism towards "the great collective identities" which traditionally have been conceived

as large-scale, all-encompassing, homogenous, as unified collective identities, which could be spoken about almost as if they
were singular actors in their own right but which, indeed, placed,
positioned, stabilized, and allowed us to understand and read,
almost as a code, the imperatives of the individual self: the great
collective social identities of class, of race, of nation, of gender,
and of the West. (Hall, "Old and New" 44)

Ultimately, these novels suggest that liberatory forms of agency are
always, to some degree, going to be in process; they are not already out
there, waiting, but must be made and remade. As Stuart Hall claims, writing of cultural identity,

It is not a fixed origin to which we can make some final and
absolute Return. Of course, it is not a mere phantasm either. It is
something—not a mere trick of the imagination. It has its histories—and histories have their real, material and symbolic effects.
The past continues to speak to us. But it no longer addresses us
as a simple, factual "past," since our relation to it, like the child's
relation to the mother, is always-already "after the break." It is
always constructed through memory, fantasy, narrative and
myth. Cultural identities are the points of identification. [. . .]
Not an essence but a *positioning*. Hence, there is always a politics
of identity, a politics of position, which has no absolute guaran-
tee in an unproblematic, transcendental "law of origin." ("Cultural Identity" 395)

This politics of identity results in a tension in the African novels. On the
one hand they insist on the need to formulate political identities that will
enable action and change. As a result, it is difficult to claim they revel in
a free play of meaning which would prevent the development of such
identities. At the same time, they often harbor the notion that collective
identity is contingent and constructed—what Hall refers to as a "positioning"—and that, as a result, forms of collective identity which are
taken as singular and fixed can silence other voices and recreate conditions
of oppression they purport to combat:

Where, then, does identity come in to [the] infinite postpone-
ment of meaning? [. . .] This is where it sometimes seems as if
Derrida has permitted his profound insights to be reappropriated

by his disciples into a celebration of formal "playfulness," which evacuates them of their political meaning. For if signification depends upon the endless repositioning of its differential terms, meaning, in any specific instance, depends on the contingent and arbitrary stop—the necessary and temporary break in the infinite semiosis of language. This does not detract from the original insight. It only threatens to do so if we mistake this "cut" of identity—this *positioning*, which makes meaning possible—as natural and permanent, rather than an arbitrary and contingent "ending." [. . .] Meaning continues to unfold, so to speak, beyond the arbitrary closure which makes it, at any moment, possible. ("Cultural Identity" 397)

Connecting this formulation of collective identity to Fanon's reflections on identity and culture in "On National Culture" can be a productive way of elaborating on the relationship between it and a liberatory political vision. Fanon claims the native intellectual will find national culture in the revolutionary collective—"the people"—who have constructed themselves:

A national culture is the whole body of efforts made by a people in the sphere of thought to describe, justify and praise the action through which that people has created itself and keeps itself in existence. (233)

The potential openness or instability suggested by the focus on the construction of the people is made explicit when Fanon claims the intellectual:

must join [the people] in that fluctuating movement which they are just giving a shape to, and which, as soon as it has started, will be the signal for everything to be called in question. Let there be no mistake about it; it is to this zone of occult instability where the people dwell that we must come. (227)

If the call to join the people urges the intellectual and cultural worker to identify with a subaltern collective, the references to the "fluctuating movement" and "zone of occult instability" in which the people are to be found suggests that the identity of this collective is necessarily always in movement and rests on shifting ground. (In fact, a primary theme running throughout "On National Culture" is a warning against seeking for a liberatory culture in a static collective identity.) This means the work of shaping an identity through action and culture is ongoing; it would be a mistake to see such work as finished, and to see identity as completed and fixed, since "the zone of occult instability where the people dwell" will always bring it "in question." This notion is also found in the African novels in this study, especially in their focus on dialogue which enables an ever more complex understanding of political struggle and, at the same time, keeps the real unstable and open for change.

These concluding reflections on political agency and identity are a logical extension of the approach to the intertextual relationships between Conrad and African fiction I have outlined in the introduction and applied in specific literary readings. My argument has been that the writing back approach limits the meaning of these relationships by situating them in a static context of anticolonial struggle with unified political/cultural agents. In contrast, the preceding intertextual readings open out the meaning of the relationships by looking at them in terms of shifting and unstable conditions of domination and resistance which complicate and bring into question accepted understandings of the political landscape and the identities they entail. This approach necessitates thinking the relationships between Conrad and African fiction in terms of contextually specific, changing patterns of convergence, divergence, and transformation. It also is profoundly influenced by Chinua Achebe, who both in his fiction and cultural criticism, embraces the idea that the meaning of cultural influences change as they are used to accommodate different historical conditions necessitating new conceptions of political and cultural identity. What we are talking about in terms of collective identity, literary production, and critical approach is the need to mediate "between old and new, between accepted norms and extravagant aberrations" (*Hopes* 65).

Notes

INTRODUCTION

1. In her well-known study *Masks of Conquest,* Gauri Viswanathan traces the ways in which a British literary curriculum was used to consolidate colonial rule. She claims that English literature, as it was taught in the colonies, encouraged the colonized to embrace an ideal Englishness and equated morality with an English code of values; as a result, literary education both masked the nature of colonial relations and resulted in an embracing of an English colonial perspective: "The introduction of English literature marks the effacement of a sordid history of colonialist expropriation, material exploitation, and class and race oppression behind European world dominance. [. . .] The English literary text, functioning as a surrogate Englishman in his highest and most perfect state, becomes a mask for economic exploitation" (20).

2. Even with *Things Fall Apart,* however, there are dangers in focusing too extensively on the notion of writing back. Most obviously, Achebe's novel does not simply assert and glorify an unproblematic Igbo culture, but emphasizes the need for change within that culture as a result of both historical circumstances and its own limitations. This complex aspect of the novel's vision can be repressed by an overly rigid focus on how it reverses the denigration of African cultures by the European colonial narrative. Less obviously, but just as importantly, an overemphasis on the novel's effort to write back can obscure the focus of *Things Fall Apart* on social concerns other than those highlighted by this effort. For example, the novel reflects critically on the politics of bourgeois African nationalism by examining the danger of African leaders who claim to speak for the community but who actually only represent their own and their class's interests. Eliding this component of the text results in a significant reduction of the richness and complexity not only of the significance of the character of Okonkwo but also of moments in the text such as the story Ekweke tells her daughter Ezinma about the tortoise and the birds, in which the tricky tortoise claims to speak for the community of birds in order to gather the best parts of a feast that has been laid

out for all of them. If the teacher or critic remains focused on approaching
Achebe's novel in terms of an effort to undermine a Western colonial narrative,
it becomes all too easy to ignore its engagement with the development of a new
form of colonialism, one which might even be able to appropriate the discourse
of African nationalism.

3. As recently as 1990, discussions of the influence of Conrad have perpetuated such Eurocentric views. In *Joseph Conrad: Third World Perspectives,* the editor Robert Hamner represents the relationships between Conrad and "Third
World" writers in terms of master and apprentice. Hamner points to "the degree
to which" these writers are "indebted" to Conrad's "example and his works" (2).
In particular, he claims, Conrad showed them "their exotic lands could be the setting for realistic drama, credible characters and relevant insights into human
nature" (1).

4. The conception of the racialized nation, fully realized in the nineteenth
century, is based on the assumptions that (1) "*every* person belongs to a race with
its own distinctive essence and its own place in the order of moral and intellectual endowments" and that (2) each race represents a nationality (Appiah 49).

5. In some cases, critics use the notion of parodic revision to continue to
construct the oppositional difference between Conrad's work and African fiction
in nativist terms; despite the cultural blending it creates, the parody is represented as upholding the value of an African culture which is utterly different
from (and perhaps better than) Western culture.

6. Achebe similarly points to how the voyage in disrupts a colonial vision
in his discussions of the way the appropriation of the novel form by African writers undermines the principles of colonialist criticism. He attacks this criticism for
insisting that African novelists must focus on the same themes and use the same
techniques as their European predecessors in order to write proper novels and
that they should be judged by the aesthetic criteria which evolved from the European literary tradition:

> we have sometimes been informed by the West and its local zealots that
> the African novels we write are not novels at all because they do not
> quite fit the specifications of that literary form which came into being
> at a particular time in specific response to the new spirit of individual
> freedom set off by the decay of feudal Europe and the rise of capitalism.
> This form, we're told, was designed to explore individual rather than
> social predicaments. (*Hopes* 54)

Dismissing this static conception of literary form, Achebe asserts that as the novel
enters into new historical and social contexts, it is necessarily transformed: "As it
happens the novel, even in its home of origin, has not behaved well; it has always
resisted the strait-jacket. What is more, being a robust art form, it has traveled
indefatigably and picked up all kinds of strange habits!" (54). He goes on to sug-

gest this type of aesthetic mutation is a form of liberation from bondage, since it represents a rejection of an authoritative, monologic vision:

> The colonialist critic, unwilling to accept the validity of sensibilities other than his own, has made a particular point of dismissing the African novel. He has written lengthy articles to prove its non-existence largely on the grounds that the novel is a particularly Western genre, a fact which would interest us if our ambition was to write "Western" novels. But in any case, did not the black people in America, deprived of their own musical instruments, take the trumpet and the trombone and blow them as they had never been blown before, as indeed they were not designed to be blown? And the result, was it not jazz? Is any one going to say that this was a loss to the world or that those first Negro slaves who began to play around with the discarded instruments of their masters should have played waltzes and foxtrots? No! (*Hopes* 89)

Achebe not only claims the aesthetic tools of the oppressor can be appropriated for purposes and traditions for which they were never intended, but he also alludes to the notion that such appropriation overturns presuppositions regarding mastery over meaning and identity.

7. In fact, it may be impossible to escape the suggestion of such evaluations when using the term influence. Clayton and Rothstein note, "Concern with influence arose in conjunction with the mid-eighteenth-century interest in originality and genius, and the concept still bears the marks of that origin" (5). As a result, the use of the term evokes notions of "charismatic figures and works" which establish their high value both through their originality and through their influence on other works of lower value—"the unoriginal, the influenced" (13).

8. *The Empire Writes Back* makes this characterization explicit, claiming: "post-colonial literatures everywhere [. . .] emerged in their present form out of the experience of colonization and asserted themselves by foregrounding the tension with the imperial power, and by emphasizing their differences from the assumptions of the imperial centre. It is this which makes them distinctively post-colonial" (2).

9. According to Miller, Africanist discourse constructs Africa as a blank. The continent comes to represent "a pure anteriority"—"the absence of time"— in which "the African mind [is] cut off from representation and signification" (169–170).

10. Gates claims the difference between these two terms does not involve the absence or presence of intention in the act of revision, "for parody and pastiche imply intention, ranging from severe critique to acknowledgment and placement within a literary tradition" (xxvii).

11. In her study of postcolonial intertextuality, *The Ballistic Bard*, Judie Newman acknowledges the need to take a "broader heteroglossic strategy" to

postcolonial texts by considering the variety of social and literary discourses to which they write back (6). Newman is concerned with the way that an exclusive focus on parodying the colonizer reinscribes "the norms of the dominant discourse with its own apparent contestation" since the very choice of that discourse for opposition reinforces its centrality (6). In order to avoid "repropogating an influence by contesting it," she asserts the need to focus on "re-reading creative adaptation from at least two traditions"; for example, she reads Shashi Tharoor's *The Great Indian Novel* in terms of both British and Indian intertexts (9). However, Newman still assumes European/postcolonial intertextuality itself is defined by the effort to write back to Western colonial discourse: the significance of the European intertext remains circumscribed by its collusive relationship with colonial discourse and the uses of transformational appropriation of those intertexts remain limited to parody.

12. Neither Nazareth nor White examine the ways Conrad reinforces colonial discourse. Nazareth does not consider them at all, and White only briefly mentions the "stereotypes" that Conrad might be read as reproducing. White goes so far as to claim, "Conrad was also one of the first writers of colonial discourse even to suggest that the formerly silenced had a voice or a point of view at all that could be, and needed to be, represented" (206). Such a statement suppresses the many ways that Conrad's representations can be read as silencing the colonial other; it is simply a reversal of the simplistic image of Conrad offered by the writing back approach.

13. As a result, these critics unintentionally risk reinforcing colonialist notions of the relationship between European and African literature since they turn Conrad into a kind of venerated spiritual ancestor from whom African authors draw inspiration and who shows these authors the path to writing decolonizing fictions.

14. For excellent discussions of the heterogeneity of European colonialism before independence, see Young and Chrisman.

15. Young objects to expanded definitions of colonialism, claiming, in particular, that forms of indirect Western domination based on influence over the native elites who run new, postindependence nations should be termed "imperialism": "Although the metaphorization of the term 'colonialism' is today being increasingly attempted on the model of the long-standing metaphorization of imperialism, for the most part it has remained resistant to such semantic expansion" (27). However, Young writes of new forms of "internal colonialism" that arose in the wake of independence, including control of the new nations by the "native bourgeois elite" whose rule results not only in continued foreign dominance but also in forms of internal, class-based colonial relationships (59). At this point Young has greatly expanded the definition of colonialism from the one he claims to be using and, for all practical purposes, imperialism and colonialism are so interwoven they cannot be separated.

16. Throughout his commentary on theories of postcolonial literatures, Ahmed himself ultimately endorses a (very traditional) socialist ur-narrative and the primacy of class as an analytic category (see *In Theory* and "The Politics of Literary Postcoloniality"). As a result, he closes off the interrogation of narratives of identity based on singular determinations which his references to "the multiplicities of intersecting conflicts based upon class, gender, nation, race, region, and so on" seem to open up.

17. Jameson briefly outlines an extremely flexible and subtle way of reading in terms of political allegory in "Third-World Literature in the Era of Multinational Capitalism":

> Our traditional conception of allegory—based, for instance, on stereotypes of Bunyan—is that of an elaborate set of figures and personifications to be read against some one-to-one table of equivalences: this is, so to speak, a one-dimensional view of this signifying process, which might only be set in motion and complexified were we willing to entertain the more alarming notion that such equivalences are themselves in constant change and transformation at each perpetual present of the text. (73)

Unfortunately, Jameson—at least in his central thesis—limits this more complex vision of how to read political allegory in "Third-World" literature by making the "nation" the collective political entity which is always being allegorized. Just as important, he claims that because "Third-World texts" are always consciously written as political allegories we must read them as such, while because of the split in Western texts between "the private and the public, between the poetic and the political" we need not read them this way (and, when we do, we are necessarily reading against the grain). Although I read the African novels in this study in terms of politics and political allegory, I do not subscribe to Jameson's vision of a split between ways of reading based on the notion that all "Third World" texts are "conscious and overt" political allegories while in "First World" texts allegorical structures can only be "unconscious" (79–80). As indicated earlier, the kind of cultural divides on which Jameson's claims are based (and so his notion of distinct theories of literature) are similar in form—if not in content—to those posited by the writing back approach. They are also equally untenable. For one thing, there are plenty of examples of political allegory in the "First World" and of "libidinal/private" texts in the "Third." More generally, this formulation ignores the ways colonialism and capitalism have sutured and divided the world in ways not addressed by a focus either on the Western colonizer/non-Western colonized divide or on the singular category of the nation.

18. James Ogude cites both the influence of Fanon and conditions in postindependence Kenya as causes for Ngugi's early sensitivity to the development of neocolonialism: "How do we account for Ngugi's radical shift in his representation of Kenyan history in his postcolonial novels? [. . .] His exposure to the works

of Marx and Fanon and the influence of a cohort group of African scholars while he was at Leeds University has been well documented. [. . .] But Ngugi was also influenced by changes taking place in the Kenyan body politic following independence. The political scenario after independence was fraught with fears and frustrations, and disillusionment with Uhuru. As early as 1966, Ngugi's bitterness was beginning to show" (10–11).

19. In this regard, as Ahmed suggests, the writing back model of analysis might work with neocolonialism by obscuring the complex structures which facilitate oppression and exploitation in postcolonial countries. Especially in terms of class structure this model often suggests that the forces to be combated are associated with the West and especially Western culture.

20. The inclusion of a novel from apartheid South Africa in this study is both justified by and points to the complexities of definitions of the colonial and the postcolonial. In the sense that South Africa was a nation which had gained its independence from direct foreign rule, *July's People,* like other novels in this study, deals with a form of colonialism (apartheid) which developed in the wake of the postcolonial nation. After all, Afrikaners "continued to see themselves as victims of English colonisation and [. . .] the imagined continuation of this victimization was used to justify the maintenance of apartheid" (Jolly 1995). Yet, to call apartheid South Africa postcolonial is, of course, in many ways perverse.

21. In *Postcolonial Con-Texts: Writing Back to the Canon,* John Thieme offers general conclusions which are, in some ways, similar to my own. Concerning efforts to categorize postcolonial appropriations of the canon, Thieme claims,

> Attractive though binary paradigms have been to some postcolonial theorists, the evidence [from his readings] invariably suggested a discursive dialectic operating along a continuum, in which the influence of the "original" could seldom be seen as simply adversarial—or, at the opposite extreme, complicitous. (2)

In his readings of these appropriations, he also notes that he strives "to keep the emphasis on the specificity of the circumstances in which particular texts have been produced" (7).

Yet, Thieme still focuses on the effort to write back, although he defines this as an effort to respond to the Western text rather than just oppose it. He is concerned with the "commonalities in the counter-discursive practice of the various texts to be considered" (2) and with the ways postcolonial texts offer readings of their Western precursors: "My purpose was, and is, simply to illustrate and analyze ways in which postcolonial writers have responded to the canonical texts in question" (13). As a result, the focus is on reading postcolonial and "canonical" texts in terms of shared concerns and purposes; the complicating differences in concerns resulting from specific, varied sociohistorical conditions remain secondary.

In his discussion of the relationships between Conrad and postcolonial fiction, this aspect of his methodology—and its difference from my own—is especially apparent. He focuses on the way "Conrad's fiction, and particularly *Heart of Darkness,* provokes a set of responses which in turn direct one back to the original novella and open up the possibility of reading it as incipiently 'postcolonial' [. . .]" (13). What this means is that intertextual relationships are still read primarily in terms of a singular, common colonial discourse and in terms of how we read Conrad in relation to this discourse (rather than in terms of the specific complex intersections and disjunctions of colonial and postcolonial conditions):

> in varying ways, each of the writers discussed in this chapter offers possibilities for dismantling polarized constructions of alterity; and finally such responses once again bring one back to Conrad and the proposition that *Heart of Darkness* itself opens up the possibility of transcending racial and other binaries. Postcolonial con-texts not only offer different perspectives in themselves, but also for readers who [. . .] mediate the story, release new meanings within their supposed pre-texts. (49)

This conclusion suggests that what is important about intertextual relationships is how they encourage us to read the canon anew; its centrality is, thus, reinforced. Ultimately, then, Thieme's reading de-emphasizes concerns in the postcolonial texts other than the effort to respond to Conrad and his engagement with a particular kind of colonialism.

CHAPTER 1

1. Ignoring entirely the links between Obi and Kurtz and focusing just on explicit references to Conrad in Achebe's novel, C.L. Innes separates Achebe from Conrad even more completely than Rogers. Innes claims "the literary models Obi frequently refers to"—especially Conrad—serve to remind "the reader of the separation between the novelist and the character he creates" (50). This perspective on Conradian references in Achebe obviously emphasize a polarity between Conrad and Achebe and denies the possibility that Achebe could have drawn on Conrad in writing *No Longer At Ease.*

2. Because of the impoverishment of their homeland resulting from the highest population density in tropical Africa, "From the 1920s Igbo artisans and clerks spread throughout Nigeria and by 1945 were increasingly prominent as well among the new generation of university graduates and ambitious businessmen" (Freund 187).

3. Achebe claims that while the Igbo value individualism greatly, they set "limits to its expression. The first limit is the democratic one, which subordinates the person to the group in practical, social matters. And the other is a moral

taboo on excess, which sets a limit to personal ambition, surrounding it with powerful cautionary tales" (*Hopes* 58). For Achebe, "the way of life which upholds the primacy of the individual" (*Hopes* 49)—which he identifies with the West—undermines a sense of the importance of community, as he illustrates in discussing the effect of a French education on the protagonist of Kane's *Ambiguous Adventure:*

> The hero of the novel, the deliverer-to-be and paragon of the new generation, returns from France a total spiritual wreck, his once vibrant sense of community hopelessly shattered. Summoned to assume the mantle of leadership, his tortured soul begs to be excused, to be left alone. "What have their problems to do with me?" he asks. "I am only myself. I have only me." Poor fellow; the West has got him! (*Hopes* 52)

He adds that in place of a "sense of community," Western individualism substitutes a very limited notion of fulfillment as "self-gratification, which is easy, short-lived and self-centered" (*Hopes* 53).

4. In his superb reading of *No Longer At Ease,* Gikandi focuses on Nigeria's unformed and liminal condition in the 50s. He claims the absence of a coherent national identity is reflected in the lack of realism in the form of the novel itself:

> Achebe sets out to do for the contemporary Nigerian scene what he did for Umuofia in *Things Fall Apart*—to evoke the transparent and representative power of narrative language, a language which will make the world available to the reader as a knowable object; but the more he tries to evoke Nigerian realities as a referent for his text, the more the new nation resists domestication in the text and hence recuperation by the reader. For when everything is said and done, Achebe's generation is trying to invent a Nigerian nation and a Nigerian national consciousness from amorphous and unstable entities arbitrarily yoked together by the colonizer. (*Reading* 80)

5. Benedict Anderson, in *Imagined Communities,* makes a strong argument for the link between, on the one hand, the rise of nationalism and a sense of national community in European colonies and, on the other, the pilgrimages necessitated by colonial educational and administrative systems (although he primarily discusses the impact of pilgrimages within colonial territory rather than to the metropolis because his argument is focused on early twentieth-century imperial policy which prevented even the most educated colonials from traveling to the metropolitan Mecca). Discussing the origins of the imagined national community in Indonesia, Anderson notes, "From all over the vast colony, but from nowhere outside it, the tender pilgrims made their inward, upward way, meeting fellow-pilgrims from different, perhaps once hostile, villages in primary school; from different ethnolinguistic groups in middle-school; and from every part of the realm in the tertiary institutions of the capital. And they knew that from wherever they had came they still had read the same books and done the same

sums. . . . To put it another way, their common experience, and the amiably competitive comradeship of the classroom, gave the maps of the colony which they studied a territorially specific imagined reality which was every day confirmed by the accents and physiognomies of their classmates" (121–122).

6. The situation of an African educated and living in Europe who writes romantic poetry brings to mind the founders of Negritude—especially Senghor. They too produced an art advocating an ideal national identity in the face of alienation and discrimination in the metropolitan center.

7. Simon Gikandi claims *No Longer At Ease* offers no real explanations for Obi's corruption and that the ignorance of all the characters at the end of the novel reflects this: "there is no resolution here, the plot has not advanced any new meanings for we are still trapped where we started, in our ignorance" (91). This is consistent with his reading of the novel in that it focuses attention on the profound ambiguity of Nigeria as a political, social, and cultural construct. However, if the chaotic, unformed Nigeria of *No Longer At Ease* resists the logic of narration, as Gikandi claims, the causes for its condition do not. The reader is not necessarily left in the same position as the characters at the end, as Gikandi suggests.

8. Abiola Irele points out that in its "comprehensive skepticism" and "uncharted nihilism," many of the fundamental principles and implications of Western poststructural thought—"the morose anti-humanism of Foucault or the corrosive intelligence of Derrida"—are incompatible with the effort of most African discourse to construct the grounds for mobilizing emancipatory energy, even though there are aspects of African intellectual and cultural production which have dovetailed with late twentieth-century Western theory (55–56). The same could be said about those intellectually corrosive aspects of European modernism—including the skepticism of Conrad—which anticipated poststructuralism.

9. Achebe's philosophical position has some important implications in terms of his literary relationship with Conrad. First, Achebe's ascription to a practical and historical approach to the notion of truth might suggest that when Achebe wrote his scathing indictments of Conrad he was not so much focused on offering a final judgment of Conrad's novel as he was on achieving a specific, historically determined goal. This goal would be the disruption of unquestioned colonialist and racist ways of reading *Heart of Darkness* in particular, and Western classics in general. This perspective on Achebe's commentary on Conrad would be supported by a statement Achebe made in response to critics of "An Image of Africa" years after it was published:

> When Achebe was told that many critics interpreted his essay as saying, "Don't read Conrad" [. . .] he explained: "It's not in my nature to talk about banning books. I am saying, read it—with the kind of understanding and with the knowledge I talk about. And read it beside African works." (Ezenwa-Ohaeto 259)

Taking a substantially less strident tone than Achebe's actual analyses of *Heart of Darkness,* this statement suggests that these analyses—including their strident tone—were intended to prod Western critics to examine their own critical assumptions. (The past twenty years of Conrad criticism suggests Achebe was successful.) Given Achebe's pragmatic and flexible approach to the notion of truth and the fact that he himself has suggested that in such essays as "An Image of Africa" his position was determined by a specific historical and rhetorical context ("An Image of Africa" was originally published in *Conradiana*), his relationship with Conrad could be more contradictory than that essay suggests without being inconsistent with his philosophical vision.

CHAPTER 2

1. This "nativist" perspective, Appiah claims, is epitomized in *Toward the Decolonization of African Literature.*

2. See Sicherman, *Ngugi wa Thiong'o: A Bibliography of Primary and Secondary Sources 1957–1987* for a comprehensive list of works (up to 1987) on the connection between Ngugi and Conrad.

3. As a result of this attraction, Ngugi chose Conrad as his "special subject" while attending Makerere University (Sicherman, "Education" 38).

4. Jabbi offers, without a doubt, the most complete exploration of the precise similarities and differences between the two novels in terms of plot and character.

5. Peter Nazareth discusses the Ngugi-Conrad connection extensively and mentions neocolonialism briefly, but he does not link the two issues.

6. It is interesting to note Jabbi is focused on the "historical experience" of the Mau Mau rebellion but pays no attention to the fact that the novel itself is focused on the historical moment of Uhuru.

7. This is Sarvan's central claim as well.

8. Although many, if not most, commentaries on *A Grain of Wheat* refer to these similarities, the analyses that explore them most fully are those by Nazareth, Sarvan, and Jabbi.

9. Of course, much contemporary criticism on Conrad focuses on the ways his texts bring into question his narrators' perspectives; however, it is difficult indeed to argue that *Under Western Eyes* undermines the contrast between Western Europe, where destructive passions are held in check, and Russia, where government and society in no way control such passions. And nowhere is there any suggestion that revolution remains anything but hopeless.

10. Kenya, like the rest of the colonized world, was severely underdeveloped by the process of colonialism. Citing the work of economist Andre Gunder Frank, Fredrick Buell points out that "Underdeveloped economies in the Third

World did not represent slow or inhibited growth toward industrial capitalism along a developmental timeline. [. . .] They weren't merely *un*-developed economies, but actively *under*developed; and this process of underdevelopment—of their exploitation by an increasingly overdeveloped global core—had begun with early colonial plunder and subjugation" (113–114).

11. The issue of arrested decolonization has, of course, been Ngugi's primary concern since the mid-Sixties. As Simon Gikandi notes, "all the novels that Ngugi has written after *A Grain of Wheat* are attempts to figure out why decolonization, which was supposed to will a new nation into being, instead produces cultures and subjects that are held hostage to the colonial past they work so hard to transcend" (*Ngugi* 127).

12. In her article "Ngugi wa Thiong'o and the Writing of Kenyan History," Carol Sicherman discusses the development of Ngugi's sense of the importance of connecting Kenyans with their history of repression and resistance (which had been usurped by colonial historiography).

13. Sicherman points out that Ngugi has a keen awareness of the way that myths and legends—especially those involving historical figures—have been imporant inspirations for action in the history of resistance ("History" 359–364).

14. Simon Gikandi insightfully writes that in *A Grain of Wheat* "the trope of arrested decolonization [. . .] should not conceal the celebratory narrative of decolonization, a powerful story of national *retour* and restoration that lies hidden under the rhetoric of failure that dominates the novel" (*Ngugi* 101). He sees the result as a "split between the romance of cultural nationalism and the disenchantment generated by a failed decolonization" (102). This split necessitates that in *A Grain of Wheat* the "ideals of cultural nationalism"—including a progressive national identity—cannot be productively perpetuated without a recognition of and effort to reduce the corrosive irony of the extant decolonization (113).

15. Nazareth points out that "[a] few weeks before Ngugi started working on his novel, he came across the work of Frantz Fanon, thanks to Grant Kamenju, who had picked up a copy of Fanon's *The Damned* (now entitled *The Wretched of the Earth*)" (243).

16. As James Ogude notes, a key aspect of Ngugi's literary project is "to salvage the history of the subaltern"—i.e. "Kenya's working people, the workers and the peasants"—suppressed by both "colonial writers and Kenya's professional or guild historians" (8–9).

CHAPTER 3

1. Makdisi assumes the novel is about the effort to move directly from imperialism to the postcolonial moment; he does not mention the possibility that there might be an intervening period of neocolonialism.

Said, on the other hand, at times offers a precise analysis of the structures and dangers of neocolonialism, focusing in particular on the need for a continuing struggle to dismantle the structures of imperialism, even after national independence has been achieved. However, when Said turns to readings of postcolonial African fiction and its relationship with Conrad, he makes no reference to neocolonialism as a pertinent issue. This could be the result of Said's focus in *Culture and Imperialism* on revealing the limitations of an imperial world view by reading texts from imperial culture in conjunction with texts from the postcolonial world.

2. The danger of ignoring Salih's own goals is reflected in Mohammad Shaheen's claim that, in comparison to Conrad's fiction, *Season of Migration* lacks clarity and has too many unresolved contradictions. Shaheen goes so far as to suggest that Conrad's "original and complex mind" was beyond Salih's understanding (169). This harsh judgment on Salih is at least in part the result of Shaheen's failure to consider Salih's specific historical and political targets.

3. For example, in *Season of Migration,* the presence and operation of Western interests is more covert that it is in *Nostromo;* the neocolony *appears* to be more independent in Salih's novel, which depicts a neocolonialism manipulated by native agents working with Western powers, rather than by Westerners manipulating the country from within (as is the case with *Nostromo*). Just as important, Salih focuses more than Conrad does on the beliefs and attitudes of the colonized themselves that allow for neocolonialism, and, in particular, on the attitudes of the masses—for example the villagers—as opposed to the native bourgeoisie.

4. See also Woodward (126, 134)

5. Abdul JanMohamed, building on Fanon's insights, has discussed colonial ideology in terms of "the Manichean allegory" which is the "central feature of the colonialist cognitive framework": "a field of diverse yet interchangeable oppositions between white and black, good and evil, superiority and inferiority, civilization and savagery, intelligence and emotion, rationality and sensuality, self and Other, subject and object" (82). He links this allegory to the perpetuation of colonial power relations: "Troubled by the nagging contradiction between the theoretical justification of exploitation and the barbarity of its actual practice, [imperial ideology] attempts to mask the contradiction by obsessively portraying the supposed inferiority and barbarity of the racial Other, thereby insisting on the profound moral difference between self and Other" (103).

6. Historically, the introduction of modern agricultural methods and technologies actually reinforced economic inequality in Sudan: "the local administrative and commercial leaders who could invest in establishing [pump schemes for the growth of cotton] soon used their positions and the power they had over tenants to enrich themselves further" (Woodward 127). However, modern commercialism was opposed where it was deemed to threaten established power: "In areas of pastoralism commercialism was met by a degree of resistance by native admin-

istrators, but this resistance was due less to the monetarisation of life itself than to the possible undermining of the autocratic local structures encouraged by imperialism" (Woodward 128).

7. Fanon remarks that "[the national bourgeoisie] will discover the need for a popular leader to whom will fall the dual role of stabilizing the regime and of perpetuating the domination of the bourgeoisie" (165).

8. Makdisi astutely notes that the end of the novel resists narrative and ideological "closure": "Rather than representing some imaginary resolution of the contradictions of form and content, *Season of Migration* leaves them gaping open" (815). Makdisi errs, however, when he assumes that we do not know whether the narrator has been saved from the river: we know the narrator survives because, in what I have called the last act of the novel, he chooses to tell the story rather than keep it secret.

Davidson's reading of the end of the novel, which is generally optimistic, fails to account fully for its subtleties: "The old oppressive order that had been in place since Islam came to the region has been disrupted" (396). Although he acknowledges that the ending "does not present a completely optimistic picture," Davidson ignores how completely it frustrates any attempt to offer final conclusions. Specifically, he does not consider how deeply infused the ideology of neocolonialism is in the narrator's consciousness and society and how crucial the acts of telling and interpretation (and so the reception of the narrator's story) are for the exposure of that ideology.

9. Yet, this appeal to the native elites in an effort to induce them to see the errors of their ways may point to a potential limitation in Salih's own conception of the means to attack neocolonialism. Ngugi has said of such appeals by writers in the early days of neocolonialism that they were ineffective because they did not account for the extent of the divisions between the new ruling classes and the majority of the peoples: "Thus the writer in this period was still limited by his inadequate grasp of the full dimension of what was really happening in the sixties: the international and national realignment of class forces and class alliances" (68).

10. Nazareth implies the narrator fully understands and overcomes the forces which control him because he is the synthesizing, self-liberating modernist artist: "The narrator understands something in himself created by colonial forces and overcomes it *through art*" ("Narrator" 124). This interpretation reinscribes the modernist relationship between narrator and audience that is, I have argued, undermined by Salih's novel. In fact, Nazareth constructs the narrator as an artist-savior: "The narrator can only perform this act of saving the people by becoming a pioneer too: *in art*" (131).

11. Nazareth claims that Conrad shatters the colonial worldview and so is a true "mental liberator," but Conrad's representations of Africans and other non-Western peoples makes such a claim highly problematic. As Ngugi has said,

"Conrad has always made me uneasy with his inability to see any possibility of redemption arising from the energy of the oppressed" (6). For many of Conrad's narrators, if there is any hope for the future it is based on the assistance that a select group of white, professional, usually British men, of which the narrator is a part, can offer to those who cannot take care of themselves—women, nonwhite people, nonprofessional European men, and so on; these groups have often been homogenized by the end of the Conradian narrative (even if the text as a whole retains the potential to undermine this homogenization).

CHAPTER 4

1. Kathrin Wagner points out that "the extent of Conrad's influence on Gordimer's work as a whole" should not be underestimated (261); and in 1977 Gordimer herself mentioned that she had "just been rereading all of Conrad" (Bazin 81). In an example of explicit influence, the protagonist of Gordimer's novel *Occasion for Loving* reads Conrad's *Victory* while on vacation by the sea. The links between the two novels, in terms of both plot and theme, are multiple.

2. It is, of course, likely Conrad's own unstable position within British culture and his history as a subaltern within the Russian empire at least partially determined his ability to question those systems. This point, however, only further reinforces the notion that one's social and political circumstances enable or limit one's capability of understanding and questioning the operation of colonial discourse.

3. This is Edward Said's term for a kind of intertextual analysis involving the scrutiny of colonial perspectives embodied in prominent metropolitan texts.

4. As C.P. Sarvan notes, "Conrad [. . .] was not entirely immune to the infection of the beliefs and attitudes of his age, but he was ahead of most in trying to break free" (285). This position is also explicitly articulated by Hawkins, Watt, and White.

5. Singh claims Marlow remains the "good colonizer" who rationalizes colonial "policies": "If blacks are evil then they must be conquered and put under white man's rule for their own good" (272).

6. I suggest, however, that the potential of *Heart of Darkness* to be read as a critique of colonial ideology could only be realized when colonial roles and practices were effectively disrupted. This point is supported by the history of criticism of *Heart of Darkness* before Achebe's scathing attack. Previously, critics did not read the novel in terms of its potential to undermine *or* support colonial ideology. They, therefore, left unquestioned the tenets of colonial ideology that Marlow—if not Conrad—perpetuates.

7. Apart from Achebe, all of the critics I mention here, whether they are indicting Conrad or defending him, acknowledge this ambivalence. Many of

them agree with Patrick Brantlinger's claim that "*Heart of Darkness* offers a powerful critique of at least certain manifestations of imperialism and racism, at the same time it presents that critique in ways which can only be characterized as both imperialist and racist" (365). Even Peter Firchow's *Envisioning Africa,* which is an extended defense of *Heart of Darkness* against Achebe and other postcolonial critics, notes the novel's "mixed" approach to imperialism (26).

    8. It also suggests the interconnection of race and class in apartheid South Africa, a point not given due consideration by many critics of the novel. In discussing the system which has formed the Smales, many critics emphasize its capitalist aspect at the expense of an analysis of the importance of apartheid. Dominic Head, for example, writes that the novel, "is a brief and powerful condemnation of consumer capitalism and the identities it creates and sustains" (123). And Rosemarie Bodenheimer goes so far as to claim that *July's People* "is largely a materialist fable in which political consciousness and identity are predicated less on race and power than on the fundamental economic facts of ownership and dispossession" (108). However, as Gordimer herself has pointed out, in apartheid South Africa, race was the primary determiner of "economic facts"—including, of course, class: "South Africa's capitalism, like South Africa's whites-only democracy, had been unlike anyone else's" ("Living" 265). In *July's People* "political consciousness and identity" *and* "ownership and dispossession" are very much "predicated [. . .] on race and power." The loss of material possessions, for the Smales, marks the loss of the power and privilege to which their white identity gave them access.

    9. In fact, there is no form of consciousness in *July's People* which has not been formed by the history of colonial policy. For example, July's wife's conception of the seasons has been determined by his infrequent visits from Johannesburg where he has had to go for work because of South African economics. In the village, when any woman's husband comes home,

> Across the seasons was laid the diuturnal one of being without a man; it overlaid sowing and harvesting, rainy summers and dry winters, and at different times, although at roughly the same intervals for all, changed for each for the short season when her man came home. For that season, although she worked and lived among the others as usual, the woman was not within the same stage of the cycle maintained for all by imperatives that outdid the authority of nature. The sun rises, the moon sets; the money must come, the man must go. (83)

There is no traditional village untouched by the effects of a system which intentionally created the necessity that its men leave in order to find work: "Mine workers had been coming from out of these places for a long, long time, almost as long as the mines had existed" (30). This is not to say there are no traditional elements left; however, in *July's People* even these elements have been utterly transformed by the impact of apartheid.

10. Remarkably, several critics of the novel duplicate Maureen's perspective on the village by assuming the existence of an untransformed traditional culture beneath the effects of apartheid. They believe that progress for July and his village involves a return to such a culture. John Cooke assumes the people of the village do not have an ordering and mapping system for their reality that is not a result of closeness to the natural landscape and that progress for the village will involve a purging of all modern, technological elements from it: "When the bakkie, symbol of life 'back there,' is finally ingested by the veld, July will no doubt fashion a new life for himself" (177). Similarly, Barbara Temple-Thurston argues July "is cut adrift from his culture" because of experiences in the city and that this disjunction and its dangers is revealed by his finding his place in the broken down hut that houses the bakkie (56). For these critics, July's village is a premodern, preindustrial locale in which the bakkie—as symbol of the technological and the urban—does not belong. To be redeemed or to remain pure July must get rid of it, and, one assumes, of all vestiges of his "urban past."

11. As Dominic Head notes, "Gordimer's point is that [. . .] ethnic African communities [. . .] are already tainted by the ideas and effects of the capitalist system, which has artificially called them into being for its own exploitative ends" (132).

12. Clingman (203) and Temple-Thurstan (58) put forward this argument as well.

13. Bart Moore-Gilbert also makes this point:

it is far from certain that the various kinds of "intransitive" resistance which Bhabha describes in his early essays debilitated colonial control in any serious way [. . .] history suggests that discourses like imperialism, fascism or homophobia are no less effective for the obvious contradictions and unconscious/affective conflicts that are inscribed in them. [. . .] Equally, there is little material evidence that psychological guerilla warfare of the kind which Bhabha describes as operating "strategically" from within the subordinate formation was, in fact, particularly destabilizing for the colonizer. (133–134)

CHAPTER 5

1. Vincent Odamtten and Gay Wilentz make similar claims about the relationship between the two novels. Commenting on the large blank spaces in the first two pages of the novel, Odamtten argues:

We are tricked, quite literally, into "the blank of whiteness"; or perhaps we are invited to take a journey opposite to Marlow's trip into *The Heart of Darkness*. The reversal of Conrad's central metaphor for the exploration of the imperial project marks Aidoo's overt departure from the aesthetic-ideological paradigm that supports that other journey. (120)

Wilentz asserts that "in [Sissie's] scathing attack on Western culture and in what she sees and contemplates in Germany," she "rejects [. . .] the notions of civilization" embedded in Conrad's "belief that culture and order existed only in Western Europe, more specifically England, and by going there one could be freed from the lack of civilization elsewhere" (83).

2. When Paula Morgan criticizes *Our Sister Killjoy* for being exclusively focused on writing back to the colonizer, she ignores its withering critique of certain kinds of nationalist and anticolonial rhetoric produced by Africans:

> The agenda seems to have been to deconstruct the master's house using his tools, or put another way, to dig up the master's gardens using his spade. The limitations of Aidoo's travel narrative is that it does not push far enough. Despite the rich allusiveness of Aidoo's shape shifting prose, the ideological confrontation between the self and the other through the travel encounter has merely been reversed. The black-eyed squint does not go much beyond overturning the white-eyed vision. (208)

3. The narrator's own ambiguous relationship with the elites is also suggested in this passage; they are referred to both in terms of difference ("they") and of identification ("we.")

4. Caroline Rooney claims Aidoo is concerned with the "matter of a creative language—a we-must-create language—that is 'African,' in its necessity at least, whether it appears in an African language or in the English one. [. . .] It is this language which would resist 'colonization'" (113). And Innes asserts that, "in seeking to change 'the way things are,' Aidoo, and her protagonist Sissie, must also challenge the way things are described, including the forms and language in which they have been described" (139).

5. Gay Wilentz both makes a claim for Sissie's allegorical relationship with a singular communal agent and, inadvertantly, suggests the problems with such a claim. She repeatedly asserts that Sissie is "the eye of her community in the land of the exiles" but also states that "she is the representative of all the mothers and sisters and daughters who have been left behind" by these exiles (81–83). Does this mean Sissie's community must be understood in strictly gendered terms? Such a reading is problematic in terms of both the book's examination of neo-colonial dynamics and of Wilentz's own discussion of those dynamics.

6. Focusing on Aidoo's engagement with nationalist political rhetoric, Elizabeth Willey claims *Our Sister Killjoy* shows a "suspicion of the rhetoric of masculinity that accompanies nationalist programs by reminding the reader that power in many contexts has been coded as masculine control over women and that this dynamic has not been challenged by nationalist thinking in Ghana" (18).

Works Cited

Achebe, Chinua. *Arrow of God.* New York: Anchor, 1964.

———. *Hopes and Impediments: Selected Essays.* New York: Anchor, 1988.

———. "An Image of Africa: Racism in Conrad's *Heart of Darkness.*" *Heart of Darkness.* Ed. Robert Kimbrough. New York: Norton, 1998. 251–62.

———. Interview with Bill Moyers. *A World of Ideas.* Ed. Betty Sue Flowers. New York: Doubleday, 1989. 333–44.

———. *No Longer at Ease.* New York: Anchor, 1960.

Ahmed, Aijaz. *In Theory: Classes, Nations, Literatures.* New York: Verso, 1992.

———. "The Politics of Literary Postcoloniality." *Race & Class* 36.3 (1995): 1–20.

Aidoo, Ama Ata. *Our Sister Killjoy.* White Plains: Longman, 1977.

Amuta, Chidi. *The Theory of African Literature: Implications for Practical Criticism.* London: Zed, 1989.

Amyuni, Mona. Introduction. Amyuni 11–25.

———, ed. *Season of Migration to the North: A Casebook.* Beirut: American UP of Beirut, 1985.

Anderson, Benedict. *Imagined Communities.* New York and London: Verso, 1983.

Appiah, Kwame Anthony. *In My Father's House.* New York: Oxford UP, 1992.

Armstrong, Paul. "*Heart of Darkness* and the Epistemology of Cultural Difference." Fincham and Hooper 21–41.

Ashcroft, Bill, Gareth Griffiths, and Helen Tiffin. *The Empire Writes Back.* New York: Routledge, 1989.

Azodo, Ada U., and Gay Wilentz, eds. *Emerging Perpsectives on Ama Ata Aidoo.* Trenton: Africa World P, 1999.

Bakhtin, M. M. *Problems of Dostoevsky's Poetics.* Trans. and ed. C. Emerson. Minneapolis: U of Minnesota P, 1984.

Bazin, Nancy, and Marilyn Seymour, eds. *Conversations with Nadine Gordimer.* Jackson: UP of Mississippi, 1990.

Bhabha, Homi. *The Location of Culture.* New York: Routledge, 1994.

Bodenheimer, Rosemarie. "The Interregnum of Ownership in *July's People.*" *The Later Fiction of Nadine Gordimer.* Ed. Bruce King. London: Macmillan, 1993. 108–20.

Boehmer, Elleke. *Colonial and Postcolonial Literature.* Oxford: Oxford UP, 1995.

Brantlinger, Patrick. "*Heart of Darkness:* Anti-Imperialism, Racism, or Impressionism?" *Criticism* 27 (1985): 363–85.

Brink, Andre. "Complications of Birth: Interfaces of Gender, Race and Class in *July's People.*" *English in Africa* 21.1–2 (1994): 157–80.

Brydon, Diana, and Helen Tiffin. *Decolonising Fictions.* Sydney: Dangaroo, 1993.

Buell, Frederick. *National Culture and the New Global System.* Baltimore: Johns Hopkins UP, 1994.

Cesaire, Aime. "From *Discourse on Colonialism.*" Williams and Chrisman 172–80.

Chinweizu, Onwuchekwa Jemie, and Ihechukwu Madubuike. *Toward the Decolonization of African Literature.* Washington: Howard UP, 1983.

Chrisman, Laura. "The Imperial Unconscious? Representations of Imperial Discourse." Williams and Chrisman 498–517.

Clayton, Jay, and Eric Rothstein, eds. *Influence and Intertextuality in Literary History.* Madison: U of Wisconsin P, 1991.

Clingman, Stephen. *The Novels of Nadine Gordimer: History from the Inside.* London: Allen & Unwin, 1986.

Conrad, Joseph. *Heart of Darkness.* Ed. Robert Kimbrough. New York: Norton, 1988.

———. *Nostromo.* New York: Penguin, 1983.

———. *Under Western Eyes.* New York: Viking Penguin, 1985.

Cooke, John. *The Novels of Nadine Gordimer: Private Lives/Public Landscapes.* Baton Rouge: Louisiana State UP, 1985.

Davidson, John. "In Search of a Middle Point: The Origins of Oppression in Tayeb Salih's *Season of Migration to the North.*" *Research in African Literatures* 20.3 (1989): 385–400.

Ezenwa-Ohaeto. *Chinua Achebe: A Biography*. Bloomington: Indiana UP, 1997.

Fanon, Frantz. *The Wretched of the Earth*. New York: Grove, 1963.

Fincham, Gail, and Myrtle Hooper, eds. *Under Postcolonial Eyes*. Cape Town: U of Cape Town P, 1996.

Firchow, Peter. *Envisioning Africa: Racism and Imperialism in Conrad's Heart of Darkness*. Lexington: UP of Kentucky, 2000.

Freund, Bill. *The Making of Contemporary Africa*. 2nd ed. Boulder: Lynne Rienner, 1998.

Gates, Henry Louis. *The Signifying Monkey*. Oxford: Oxford UP, 1988.

Ghandi, Leela. *Postcolonial Theory: A Critical Introduction*. New York: Columbia UP, 1998.

Gikandi, Simon. *Ngugi wa Thiong'o*. Cambridge: Cambridge UP, 2000.

———. *Reading Chinua Achebe*. Portsmouth: Heinemann, 1991.

Gordimer, Nadine. *July's People*. New York: Penguin, 1981.

———. "Living in the Interregnum." *The Essential Gesture*. Ed. Stephen Clingman. New York: Penguin, 1988. 261–84.

Gurnah, Abdulrazak, ed. *Essays on African Writing 1: A Re-evaluation*. Westport: Heinemann, 1994.

Hall, Stuart. "Cultural Identity and Diaspora." *Colonial Discourse and Post-Colonial Theory*. Williams and Chrisman 392–403.

———. "Old and New Identities, Old and New Ethnicities." *Culture, Globalization, and the World-System*. Ed. Anthony King. Minneapolis: U of Minnesota P, 1997. 41–68.

———. "When Was 'The Post-Colonial'? Thinking at the Limit." *The Post-Colonial Question*. Eds. Iain Chambers and Lidia Curti. New York: Routledge, 1996. 242–60.

Hamner, Robert, ed. *Joseph Conrad: Third World Perspectives*. Washington: Three Continents, 1990.

Hawkins, Hunt. "The Issue of Racism in *Heart of Darkness*." *Conradiana* 14.3 (1982): 163–71.

Head, Dominic. *Nadine Gordimer*. Cambridge: Cambridge UP, 1994.

Hulme, Peter. "The Locked Heart: The Creole Family Romance of *Wide Sargasso Sea*." *Colonial Discourse/Postcolonial Theory*. Eds. Francis Barker, Peter Hulme, and Margaret Iversen. New York: Manchester UP, 1994. 72–88.

Hyam, Ronald. *Britain's Imperial Century, 1815–1914*. Lanham: Barnes and Noble, 1993.

Innes, C. L. *Chinua Achebe*. Cambridge: Cambridge UP, 1990.

——— . "Conspicuous Consumption: Corruption and Body Politic in the Writing of Ayi Kwei Armah and Ama Ata Aidoo." *Essays on African Writing 2*. Ed. Abdulrazak Gurnah. Portsmouth: Heinemann, . 1–18.

——— . "Mothers or Sisters? Identity, Discourse and Audience in the Writing of Ama Ata Aidoo and Mariama Ba." Nasta 127–51.

Irele, Abiola. "Dimensions of African Discourse." *College English* 19.3 (1992): 45–59.

Jabbi, Bu-Buakei. "Conrad's Influence on Betrayal in *A Grain of Wheat*." *Research in African Literatures* 11 (1980): 50–83.

Jackson, Thomas. "Orality, Orature, and Ngugi wa Thiong'o." *Research in African Literatures* 22 (1991): 5–15.

Jameson, Fredric. "Third-World Literature in the Era of Multinational Capitalism." *Social Text* 15 (1986): 65–88.

JanMohamed, Abdul. "The Economy of Manichean Allegory: The Function of Racial Difference in Colonialist Literature." *"Race," Writing, and Difference*. Ed. Henry Louis Gates Jr. Chicago: U of Chicago P, 1985. 78–106.

——— . *Manichean Aesthetics: The Politics of Literature in Colonial Africa*. Amherst: U of Massachusetts P, 1983.

Jolly, Rosemary. "Rehearsals of Liberation: Contemporary Postcolonial Discourse." *PMLA* 110.1 (1995): 17–29.

Julien, Eileen. *African Novels and the Question of Orality*. Bloomington: Indiana UP, 1992.

Korang, Kwaku. "Ama Ata Aidoo's Voyage Out: Mapping the Coordinates of Modernity and African Selfhood in *Our Sister Killjoy*." *Kunapipi* 14.3 (1992): 50–61.

Kristeva, Julia. *Desire in Language: A Semiotic Approach to Literature and Art*. Ed. Leon S. Roudiez. Trans. Thomas Gora, Alice Jardine, and Leon S. Roudiez. New York: Columbia UP, 1980.

Loomba, Ania. *Colonialism/Postcolonialism*. New York: Routledge, 1998.

Makdisi, Saree S. "The Empire Renarrated: *Season of Migration to the North* and the Reinvention of the Present." *Critical Inquiry* 18 (1992): 804–20.

Maughan-Brown, David. *Land Freedom and Fiction: History and Ideology in Kenya*. London: Zed, 1985.

McClintock, Anne. "The Angel of Progress: Pitfalls of the Term 'Post-colonialism.'" Williams and Chrisman 291–305.

——— . *Imperial Leather*. New York: Routledge, 1995.

Miller, Christopher. *Blank Darkness: Africanist Discourse in French*. Chicago: U of Chicago P, 1985.

Miller, J. Hillis. "*Heart of Darkness* Revisited." *Conrad Revisited: Essays from the Eighties*. Ed. Ross C. Murfin.U of Alabama P, 1985. 31–50.

Mnthali, Felix. "Continuity and Change." *Kunapipi* 3 (1981): 91–109.

Moore-Gilbert. *Postcolonial Theory: Contexts, Practices, Politics*. New York: Verso, 1997.

Morgan, Paula. "The Risk of (Re)membering My Name: Reading *Lucy* and *Our Sister Killjoy* as Travel Narratives." Azodo and Wilentz 187–211.

Mukherjee, Arun P. "Whose Post-Colonialism and Whose Postmodernism." *World Literature Written in English* 30.2 (1990): 1–9.

Nasta, Susheila, ed. *Motherlands*. New Brunswick: Rugers UP, 1992.

Nazareth, Peter. "Is *A Grain of Wheat* a Socialist Novel?" *Critical Perspectives on Ngugi wa Thiong'o*. Ed. G.D. Killam. Washington: Three Continents, 1984. 243–64.

———. "The Narrator as Artist and the Reader as Critic." Amyuni 123–34

———. "Out of Darkness: Conrad and Other Third World Writers." Hamner 217–31.

Newman, Judie. *The Ballistic Bard*. New York: Arnold, 1995.

Ngugi wa Thiong'o. *A Grain of Wheat*. Portsmouth: Heinemann, 1967.

———. *Moving the Center*. Portsmouth: Heinemann, 1993.

Niblock, Tim. *Class and Power in Sudan*. Albany: State U of New York P, 1987.

Nkrumah, Kwame. *Hands Off Africa!!! Some Famous Speeches by Dr. The Right Honorable Kwame Nkrumah*. Ed. Kwabena Owusu-Akyem. Accra: Ministry of Local Government, 1960.

Obumselu, Ebele. "*A Grain of Wheat*: Ngugi's Debt to Conrad." *Critical Perspectives on Ngugi wa Thiong'o*. Ed. G.D. Killam. Washington: Three Continents, 1984. 110–121.

Ogude, James. *Ngugi's Novels and African History*. Sterling: Pluto, 1999.

Odamtten, Vincent O. *The Art of Ama Ata Aidoo*. Gainesville: U of Florida P, 1994.

Rogers, Philip. "*No Longer At Ease*: Chinua Achebe's 'Heart of Whiteness.'" *Postcolonial Literatures: Achebe, Ngugi, Desai, Walcott*. Ed. Michael Parker and Roger Starkey. New York: St. Martin's P, 1995. 53–63.

Rooney, Caroline. "'Dangerous Knowledge' and the Poetics of Survival: A Reading of *Our Sister Killjoy* and *A Question of Power*." Nasta 99–126.

Sackey, Edward. "Oral Tradition and the African Novel." *Modern Fiction Studies* 37 (1991): 389–407.

Said, Edward. *Culture and Imperialism.* New York: Knopf, 1993.

Salih, Tayeb. *Season of Migration to the North.* Portsmouth: Heinemann, 1969.

Sarvan, C.P. "Racism and the *Heart of Darkness.*" *Heart of Darkness.* Ed. Robert Kimbrough. New York: Norton, 1988. 280–85.

Sarvan, Ponnuthurai. "Under African Eyes." Hamner. 153–60.

Seton-Watson, Hugh. *Nations and States: An Enquiry into the Origins of Nations and the Politics of Nationalism.* Boulder: Westview, 1977.

Shaheen, Mohammad. "Tayeb Salih and Conrad." *Comparative Literature Studies* 22:1 (1985): 156–71.

Sicherman, Carol. "Ngugi's British Education." *Ngugi wa Thiong'o: Texts and Contexts.* Trenton: Africa World, 1995. 35–46.

———. "Ngugi wa Thiong'o and the Writing of Kenyan History." *Research in African Literatures* 20 (1989): 347–70.

———. *Ngugi wa Thiong'o: A Bibliography of Primary and Secondary Sources 1957–1978.* London: Zell, 1989.

Singh, Frances. "The Colonialstic Bias of *Heart of Darkness.*" *Heart of Darkness.* Ed. Robert Kimbrough. New York: Norton, 1988. 268–80.

Spivak, Gayatri Chakravorty. "Can the Subaltern Speak?" Williams and Chrisman 66–111.

Spurr, David. *The Rhetoric of Empire.* Durham: Duke UP, 1993.

Temple-Thurston, Barbara. "Madam and Boy: A Relationship of Shame in Gordimer's *July's People.*" *World Literature in English* 28:1 (1988): 51–58.

Thieme, John. *Postcolonial Con-Texts: Writing Back to the Canon.* New York: Continuum, 2001.

Viswanathan, Gauri. *Masks of Conquest.* New York: Columbia UP, 1989.

Wagner, Kathrin. *Rereading Nadine Gordimer.* Bloomington: Indiana UP, 1994.

Watt, Ian. "Conrad's *Heart of Darkness* and the Critics." *North Dakota Quarterly* 57.3 (1989): 5–15.

White, Andrea. "Conrad's Legacy in Postcolonial Literature." *Under Postcolonial Eyes.* Fincham and Hooper 195–208.

———. *Joseph Conrad and the Adventure Tradition.* Cambridge: Cambridge UP, 1993.

Wilentz, Gay. "The Politics of Exile: Reflections of a Black-Eyed Squint in *Our Sister Killjoy.*" *Emerging Perspectives on Ama Ata Aidoo.* Azodo and Wilentz 79–92.

Willey, Elizabeth. "National Identities, Tradition, and Feminism: The Novels of Ama Ata Aidoo Read in the Context of the Works of Kwame Nkrumah." *Interventions: Feminist Dialogues on Third World Women's Literature and Film.* Eds. Bishnupriya Ghosh and Brinda Bose. New York: Garland, 1997. 3–30.

Williams, Patrick, and Laura Chrisman, eds. *Colonial Discourse and Post-Colonial Theory.* New York: Columbia UP, 1994.

Woodward, Peter. *Sudan, 1898–1989.* Boulder: Lynne Rienner, 1990.

Young, Robert. *Postcolonialism.* Malden: Blackwell, 2001.

Index

abrogation, 2
Achebe, Chinua: on appropriation,
  142n. 6; *Arrow of God,* 35–36; on
  Conrad, 3, 31, 94, 149–50n. 9; on
  cultural influence, 140; elitism
  and, 48; on Igbo culture, 34–36,
  46–47, 147–48, n. 3; *Image of
  Africa,* 3, 31, 94, 149–50n. 9;
  "Named for Victoria, Queen of
  England" 47; on the novel,
  142–43n. 6; *Things Fall Apart,*
  5–6, 141–42n. 2. See also *No
  Longer at Ease*
African literature: colonialism in/and,
  2–5, 21–25; colonialist model of,
  6–7, 13, 142n. 6; Conrad and,
  2–6, 8, 10, 15–17; nativist model
  of, 8–9, 49; orature and, 8; writing
  back model of, 2, 5–6, 12
African-American literature, 10
agency, 19–21, 137–40; in *Our Sister
  Killjoy,* 132–34
Ahmed, Aijaz, 14, 20, 22, 145n. 16,
  146n. 19
allegory, 19–20, 145n. 17
Ambiguous Adventure (Kane), 148n. 3
Amuta, Chidi, 6–7, 8, 9
Anderson, Benedict, 54, 148–49n. 5
apartheid: and colonialism, 146n. 20;
  Gordimer on, 89, 155n. 8; in *July's
  People,* 27, 89–92, 98–108

Appiah, Kwame, 7, 9, 49, 150n. 1
appropriation, 2–5, 10, 142n. 6; in *A
  Grain of Wheat,* 52–53, 63–64,
  66–67. See also hybridity; revision;
  writing back model
Armstrong, Paul, 95
Arrow of God (Achebe), 35–36

Bakhtin, M.M., 11, 21
Ballistic Bard (Newman), 143–44n.
  11
Bhabha, Homi, 92, 93, 96–97, 103,
  107, 137
bildungsroman, 111–13, 133
black-eyed squint, 124–25, 132
Bloom, Harold, 10–11
Bodenheimer, Rosemarie, 90, 155n. 8
Boehmer, Elleke, 15
bolekaja critics, 8
Brantlinger, Patrick, 155n. 7
Brink, Andre, 106
Brydon, Diana, 10, 13
Buell, Frederick, 49, 63, 150–51n. 10

capitalism: in *A Grain of Wheat,*
  57–59; in *July's People,* 155n. 8; in
  Our Sister Killjoy, 119–24, 127–28
Cesaire, Aime, 78
Clayton, Jay, 7, 143n. 7
Clingman, Steven, 156n. 12
colonial discourse analysis, 22

167